Victorian Treasures

Victorian Treasures

BY

CAROL McD. WALLACE

PHOTOGRAPHY BY

MARIA FERRARI

ABRADALE PRESS

HARRY N. ABRAMS, INC., PUBLISHERS

PRODUCER:
Judy Fireman

DESIGN BY:
Our Designs, Inc.

ART DIRECTION:
Natasha Lessnik

BACKGROUND PAINTINGS:
Joy Nagy

PHOTOGRAPHER'S
ASSISTANT:
Krista Williams

LIBRARY OF CNGRESS
CATALOGING-IN-PUBLICATION DATA
WALLACE, CAROL 1955–
VICTORIAN TREASURES : AN ALBUM AND
HISTORICAL GUIDE FOR COLLECTORS
/BY CAROL MCD. WALLACE ; PHOTOGRAPHY BY MARIA FERRARI.
P.   CM.
ORIGINALLY PUBLISHED: NEW YORK : H.N. ABRAMS, C 1993.
INCLUDES BIBLIOGRAPHICAL REFERENCES AND INDEX.
ISBN 0–8109–8149–1
1. VICTORIANA—COLLECTORS AND COLLECTING—UNITED STATES.
2. VICTORIANA IN INTERIOR DECORATION.   I. FERRARI, MARIA.
II. TITLE.

NK807.W35 1996
745'.09'034075—DC20   96-3895

THIS 1996 EDITION IS PUBLISHED BY
HARRY N. ABRAMS, INCORPORATED, NEW YORK
A TIMES MIRROR COMPANY

Printed and bound in Italy

Table of Contents

About This Book

*V*ictorian Treasures is not the kind of collector's guide that analyzes a set of objects and supplies information about identification, condition, and prices. Nor is it a book about how to buy Victorian antiques. It is something different. Judy Fireman, the book's creator, and I have sought to present here a sampling of beautiful and interesting Victorian objects along with information about how those objects functioned in their day.

First, to define our terms. In the trade, an "antique" is defined either as an object more than one hundred years old, or, more traditionally, as any object securely datable before 1830 (therefore, before the beginning of the industrial revolution and the commencement of mass production). Not everything sold in the antiques business, however, falls into these divisions. Many stores and antiques fairs also offer "collectibles." This term often refers to the newly valuable—objects not previously considered "antiques" of lasting value. The term "collectible" also denotes objects of lesser monetary value. Simply put, collectibles cost less than big-ticket antiques.

We have included both "antiques" and "collectibles" in this book. You will find highly ornate, handcrafted objects that were extravagantly expensive when they were made and that are even more valuable today—such as silver tableware from Tiffany and Co. On the other hand, you will also find everyday, machine-made domestic tools, such as steel knives and a cast-iron coffee mill. Our aim has been to survey Victorian life, not to establish levels of value.

We have, however, made other rules in our selection process. We have ruled out the categories that specialist collectors concentrate on, such as furniture and most textiles (including rugs and linens). Therefore, you won't find coins or paper scrap in this book. Nor will you find toy soldiers, stamps, or clothing. There are a few exceptions. Books appear once, in their decorative capacity. We have also included three pieces of jewelry, as examples of the quintessentially Victorian pastime, hair craft.

Our goal throughout is to help you understand how these pieces came into being and how they were used. The book is organized room by room to provide a sense of how these articles fit into the life of a Victorian home. If you can imagine a courting couple sitting in front of a parlor fireplace, looking at "views" in a stereopticon, that adds a level of enjoyment and imaginative participation to your ownership of such an object.

We have placed objects in the rooms where they were used, but some articles with less specialized purposes, such as trays, vases, or candlesticks, might have been found in almost any room. We also made every effort to include a similar number of items from each room. Practical issues interfered, however. The Victorians made an enormous number of things, but some lasted longer than others. The more expensive and formal items, of course, have held up well. Silver survives better than glass. Because the parlor and the dining room were the principal settings for the middle-class Victorian display of prosperity, there are lots of decorative objects related to entertaining and eating in this book. On the other hand, the chapter on the nursery is shorter, partly because nurseries were furnished with less profusion than is generally imagined, partly because their contents received very hard wear, and partly because the least-favored items in a house often ended up being relegated to the children's quarters. These were often serviceable but old-fashioned things from elsewhere in the house, such as simple Queen Anne chairs or curtained bedsteads with the curtains cut off.

Thrift was a cornerstone of Victorian values, so things weren't thrown away without good reason. Amid the clutter of the average Victorian parlor, you might find the very latest in feather sculpture next to Great-Aunt Emma's Regency teacups. Rare indeed was the housewife who was willing to scrap everything in her parlor just to be fashionable.

The chronological scope of this book thus covers more than simply the dates of Queen Victoria' reign (1837 to 1901). Most objects here were produced between 1850 and 1900, but a few date from outside of that fifty-year span. Objects made before 1837 were highly likely to be in use after Victoria's coronation; similarly, no one changed household fittings just because the century turned, so many of the objects included here were still in use after 1900. We have tried however, to confine our selections to objects manufactured before 1900.

It is not always possible to date objects exactly, and we have made no attempt in that direction when stylistic or other evidence does not give us any clues. The captions below the photographs contain the most accurate information we could gather. We use "circa" to cover an estimated ten-year span, and where we have been unable to uncover more certain information, we have made no guesses. Many captions date objects as "late nineteenth century" because we could not be more precise with any real authority.

Our policy regarding country of origin is similar. The principal focus of *Victorian Treasures* is American and English goods. However, international trade was already in full swing at mid-century, so the middle-class parlor in Peoria was entirely likely to contain porcelain from France, glass from Venice, or a paper Japanese fan. Where the origin (or manufacturer) of the objects photographed is known, we have given it, and where it is unknown, it is left out.

Most of the articles in this book are in the mainstream Victorian taste. With a few exceptions, we have not included examples of the Aesthetic, Arts and Crafts, and Art Nouveau movements. Although they strongly affected average middle-class taste by the late 1880s, in their purest form they were rather elitist and remained separate from the general run of household objects.

While there are many beautiful Victorian objects in museums all over America and Europe, there are also many beautiful Victorian objects in the hands of private collectors and dealers, many of whom generously loaned their treasures to be photographed for this book. Private collectors ("Collection Anthony Trollope") and dealers or galleries ("Antiques for Sale") are listed by name in the captions. Addresses, phone numbers and summary information about the dealers and their offerings are available in the *List of Sources* section at the back of the book.

We are grateful to all of our contributors, and to many others, for their generosity of spirit and their commitment to good books. Our special thanks to the following: Michael Cipriano, Mark Clayton, Ellen Israel, Nedra and Louis Kleinman, Lauren Kearns, Wendy Matthews, Steve Mohr, Max Midroit, Gary Parks, T&T Woodworking, Randy Tibbott, and Paul Gottlieb and Eric Himmel at Harry N. Abrams.

Introduction

Only fifty years ago, today's passion for the Victorian era and all its relics would have been considered laughable. If the artifacts of the 1939 World's Fair were the acme of good taste ("streamlined," "geometric," and "functional"), then a massive silver pitcher in the form of a statuesque lady's head could only look ridiculous.

But here at its end, our century's enchantment with modernism is fading. For every glorious, sleek Seagram Building, we have seen hundreds of featureless skyscrapers. For every neatly functional nest of rimless mixing bowls, we have seen hundreds of objects whose lack of detail seems skimpy. "Space-age," in the 1990s, smacks perilously of the silly Jetsons. We want no more of it.

We want plush. We want ruffles. We want fringe, rosebuds, and ornately carved edges. We want cut-glass inkwells and round walnut tables with marble tops. We want picture frames studded with garlands of gilded plaster fruit. We want upholstery that yields when one sinks into it. We want paisley shawls. We want, in fact, what our forefathers wanted some hundred years ago.

It's not hard to see why. From our post-Freud, post-Marx vantage point, the world looks a little bleak. We probably wouldn't actually give up our twentieth-century freedoms and conveniences, but the Victorian world sometimes makes us a little wistful. We imagine it, accurately or not, as more secure, more optimistic, less ruthless than the times we live in. Wouldn't it be nice, for instance, to really believe in Manifest Destiny, to be sure that America is always right? To be sure that staying home with your children is the right thing to do? To know your bank manager by name?

It is important to realize that our view of the economics of the Victorian era is more than a little skewed. A good many more people lived downstairs than up. Wealth, ever more attractive than poverty, is overrepresented in movies and television, and it's very easy to forget the less alluring aspects of the Victorian era: the illnesses, the poverty, the labor injustices, even the chilly winter temperature of a New England bedroom.

Nevertheless, one facet of our nostalgia is not misplaced. The middle class did live, a hundred years ago, with an amplitude that we can rightfully envy. In 1880, it cost around $3,750 to build a ten-room house in America. One rough but commonly used rule of thumb for converting nineteenth-century dollars to today's value is to multiply

by thirty-five, which would bring the figure to $131,250. That would be a marvelous bargain today for a ten-room house built on the Victorian scale. And the house would have been filled, as a matter of course, with items that seem luxurious refinements today. To their credit, the Victorians established new standards of comfort that have not yet been surpassed, and though technology has added fillips like Jacuzzis to immense bathtubs, immense bathtubs were Victorian to begin with. It's no accident that the style of the modern world's most comfortable and expensive hotels is Victorian.

The Victorian Revival

Of course, the appeal of the Victorian era is not merely that of nostalgia. Great American fortunes were made a hundred years ago, and some of that money is still around, paying yacht club dues and watering broad green lawns in expensive ZIP codes. The 1980s saw the consolidation of a number of new fortunes, and many of the new ultra-rich embraced Victorian style. Because it was old, it gave them legitimacy. The nineteenth-century robber barons, who lined their rooms with paneling pulled from centuries-old English manor houses, had already established that fact. In recent years, the paraphernalia of a prosperous past has been flung around to create a stage set for more than one social fantasy.

What's more, Victorian style means lushness and lavishness. It is innately showy. After all, as a style that was itself formed by nouveaux riches, its rediscovery a hundred years later is completely logical. And while very few people acknowledge that they decorate their homes with an eye to what's fashionable in the upper classes, the rash of opulently decorated rooms depicted in interior design magazines has brought attention to a style that had long been neglected, and that now looks good.

This is an essential factor in the current Victorian revival. To our eyes, long starved for detail, Victoriana represents a feast. After a steady diet of beige and right angles, we cannot get enough crimson and floral carving. And although most of the surviving artifacts of the Victorian age were machine-produced (which is why there are so many of them), they were made to a much better standard than we are used to now. Even if the aesthetics of a Gothic revival sideboard appall you, you have to admire the workmanship.

To understand the sheer profusion of the Victorian style, it helps to look back at eighteenth century society. The eighteenth century was the great era of aristocracy. In Europe, a handful of men controlled not only government and vast wealth, but information. Culture lay in the laps of a tiny percentage of the population. The average farmer couldn't read. The average carpenter never traveled beyond his provincial town. News was spread by broadsheet and word of mouth. Ships took months to cross an ocean. For most of the population, life was a fairly hermetic affair.

It was also plain. Food was plain, clothes were plain. So were houses. The prevailing aristocratic style of the eighteenth century might have been elaborate, but as the style trickled down to affect an armchair in rural Virginia or distant Yorkshire, this meant only that the legs might curve, if the local joiner were skillful enough. The ornate carving, elaborate ormolu, inlaid porcelain plaques, and complex marquetry that we know from museum pieces did not exist for the common man. He simply never saw them. And what he might have seen—the more modest bourgeois version of high style—was still out of his reach.

And then, with a puff of steam and a clatter of gears, the industrial revolution changed everything.

The Rise of the Bourgeoisie

In the late eighteenth and early nineteenth centuries, the middle class was composed of the most prosperous farmers and tradesmen and a small group of managers and professionals: doctors, lawyers, bankers. But as industrialization concentrated production into factories, the middle class expanded enormously. The number of men who wore white collars and suits to work and spent their days behind a desk increased dramatically in

America, from 750,000 in 1860 to 2,160,000 in 1890 and 4,420,000 in 1910.

These men worked predominantly in cities. They left their houses in the morning, often taking a trolley car to work from one of the new "suburbs" outside of the commercial center of town. And they earned salaries that not only fed and clothed their families, but provided some discretionary income. There wasn't much to spend this discretionary income on in those days: no expensive hobbies, no lavish restaurant meals or fast cars. So many Victorian families spent money on decorating their homes.

They were helped enormously in this enterprise by developments in merchandising, most notably the rise of the department store. The first consumer palace was opened in New York in 1862 by A. T. Stewart, and it exhibited many innovative merchandising features that we now take for granted. Prices were fixed; shoppers need no longer bargain for goods. All customers were treated with the same courtesy, be they Fifth Avenue matrons or sweatshop girls from the Lower East Side.

Best of all, a previously unimaginable range of merchandise was constantly on alluring, tempting display. This was perhaps the most significant change, because it marked a crucial transition in consumer attitudes. No longer did one shop to fill a need; one shopped to satisfy a desire. Where the housewife of 1830 would buy a new tablecloth from the dry-goods emporium because she could no longer mend the holes in the old one, the housewife of 1880 would buy a new tablecloth because she had seen it on the counter at Wanamaker's and the new two-tone damask would look so splendid with her china.

The new middle classes would not have known what to buy, however, without the contemporaneous acquisition of information. Advances in printing technology coincided with advances in literacy to fuel the explosion of the popular press in the late nineteenth century. Frank Leslie's *Illustrated Newspaper*, founded in 1855, livened up gray pages of print with highly detailed woodcut illustrations. *Godey's Lady's Book*, founded in 1830, attracted new readers and became something of an oracle for its middle-class audience, along with its principal competitor, *Harper's Bazar*. The advertisers whose goods appeared in those pages had a powerful influence on the formation of taste. So did decorating advice from "authorities" appearing in magazine and newspaper columns as well as in a flood of books by authors such as Charles Eastlake and Mrs. M. E. W. Sherwood.

Indeed, the Victorian consumer needed help. This fertile period of technical innovation brought an intoxicating confusion of choice to the home decorating field. Suddenly, objects that had been available only to the rich were accessible to the ordinary householder, in approximate versions, at least. For example, in the 1830s, new machines were developed to cut thin veneers of precious woods. It became possible to lay a skin of mahogany over a frame of pine and sell the resulting piece of furniture quite cheaply, bringing the look of solid mahogany within the reach of the modest purse. The jacquard loom mechanically produced a kind of brocade. Parian ware imitated hard-paste porcelain. Pressed glass looked almost like cut glass, and roller-printing on wood-pulp paper made decorated walls positively cheap.

However dizzying the choice among furnishing items may have been, certain assumptions run throughout the advice literature of the era. For the first time in history, houses were divided into single-use rooms: bedrooms, kitchen, dining room. As soon as a family could afford to, it would furnish one room with a "suite" of matched furniture and label it the "parlor." Greater prosperity brought on a building boom, and soon families could devote a room to a nursery, a library, possibly even a boudoir, or ladies' sitting room. A typical seven-room "Queen Anne" house of the mid-eighties, complete with a "picturesque" non-functioning tower, contained three bedrooms, dining room, kitchen, parlor, and a less formal sitting room. It was commodious, but not grand. Its urban equivalent, the brownstone or terraced house, would attempt to compress similarly specialized rooms into the confines of a city lot.

One feature of domestic arrangements, however, that was present less often than we (perhaps wistfully) imagine was servants' quarters. Reliable studies estimate that the number of urban American households with live-in servants hovered around twenty-five percent for most of the Victorian era. (In England, where democratic aspirations and lucrative manufacturing jobs didn't exist to the same extent, servants were easier to come by.) These statistics do not, of course, include daily help, which was common, and families that could afford to often sent laundry and ironing out to be done in someone else's home. Even so, the work load was mind-boggling. One scholar estimates that the average housewife spent twenty-seven hours a week cleaning her home.

Standards, of course, were high. Cleanliness was next to godliness. Dingy curtains or dusty tabletops implied moral decay, and a woman who tolerated them must be a slattern, as careless with her principles as she was with her mop. Readers of Victorian novels know that the lingering odor of cabbage in a hallway stands for squalor.

Cleanliness was not the only issue on which housekeepers were judged. As soon as most middle-class men did their work outside the home, a firm line of demarcation was drawn between the world of commerce and the world of domesticity. Man inhabited the former, woman the latter. And once a wife no longer contributed to the family's financial well-being, her regulation of domestic affairs became the primary reflection of her identity. As the Victorian commentator Frances Power Cobbe put it, "The more womanly a woman is, the more she is sure to throw her personality over the home . . . and transform it . . . into a sort of outermost garment of her soul." This meant crisp linens, sweet-smelling rooms, waxed furniture, glittering windows, timely meals, mannerly children. It also meant owning the right stuff.

Correct Taste

Homes and their contents have always made statements about wealth and social status. And in times like the Victorian period when social lines were shifting, the material manifestations of status became increasingly important. If you are a small-town banker and your father was a farmer, establishing your bourgeois rank is important. And in 1850, you could do this with roses.

The earliest full-blown "Victorian" style was lush in the extreme. The typical artifact might be a love seat built by German-American cabinetmaker John Henry

Belter, who invented a process of laminating, steaming, and carving layers of rosewood to produce extraordinarily elaborate rococo revival furniture. The back of a chair would rise above the upholstery like a Spanish hair comb, carved into a bouquet of roses or a fruit-filled cornucopia. In the 1850s carving spoke of manual labor and great expense. The glossy finish that was standard in those days was imparted by varnish, often known in England as "French polish." A mirror-bright finish on a table implied the regular ministrations of a housemaid.

Many of the finest Belter pieces are upholstered in deeply buttoned fabric. Once sprung cushions were devised in the 1820s, softer, more luxurious upholstery became economically available to the middle class. The buttons, as well as adding ornament, stressed just how deep the stuffing went. New fabric-dyeing technology also made more colors available, and the mid-Victorians loved color. Until early in the century, soft-hued vegetable dyes had predominated, but mineral and aniline colorings produced mid-century provided highly popular magentas and turquoises, clear strong colors with the appeal of novelty.

So all in all, a Belter love seat (or a less ambitious piece in Belter's style) was the embodiment of taste and quality that had previously been the prerogative of the wealthy. The same was true of many of the objects so popular at mid-century: the wallpapers patterned with nodding bouquets of blossoms, the massive gilt-framed mirrors, the color reproductions of famous paintings.

The Aesthetic Decades

Fashions changed, naturally, in the course of the Victorian era. The glowing colors and curvilinear outlines of mid-century gave way to browns and olives and massive, blocky oak pieces. The large-scaled, shaded, naturalistic patterns so sought after in the 1850s and '60s were discarded for flat, abstract motifs. These changes were promoted by a group of design reformers that included Englishmen Charles Eastlake and William Morris, who found much of exuberant mid-Victorian taste to be "meaningless" and "decadent."

William Morris believed that Victorian interiors were too cluttered and urged householders to select their ornaments more carefully. But even the strictest "reformed" or "Aesthetic" interior (one designed according to these new aesthetic precepts) looks ornate to eyes accustomed to modernism. Morris, after all, suggested using several chintz patterns in one room. Eastlake urged readers to acquire pieces of porcelain, ivory, or Venetian glass to mass in an ornamental fashion over a mantel. Literal, total plainness still smacked too much of poverty to be an acceptable decorating motif.

Although some people swallowed this dogma in its entirety and decorated their houses in the strictest of reformed taste, most did not. What's more, home furnishings have a permanence that discourages the average householder from embracing ideological trends. If you purchased a mahogany-veneered four-piece parlor suite in 1866, you are not going to put it on the bonfire in 1870 just because Charles Eastlake says it belongs there. In reality, as we can see from period photographs, the solid oak furniture of the 1870s and '80s often shared the same hearth with the crimson velvet of an earlier decade, while a hand-hammered silver sugar basin with exposed rivets sat next to rose-strewn saucers on the tea tray.

Styles changed, but the prevailing attitude did not. More was still more, and Victorian consumers were involved in a love affair with material goods that we, who take profusion for granted, are hard put to understand. It is difficult to find a modern analogy, for instance, for their appreciation of novelty. So little in our world is new or even strange. But when Japan reopened trade with the West, the artifacts of that insular culture were snapped up eagerly. Cherry blossoms replaced roses on teacups. Stereopticon views showed men in kimonos and women with deformed feet, strange-looking palaces and gnarled little trees. No one had ever seen anything like it before. That is an innocence we cannot recapture.

The exoticism of Japanese goods had a pronounced effect on end-of-century aesthetics. By the 1880s, the Japanese fan had become a commonplace decorating accessory, and asymmetrical Oriental designs appeared wholesale on wallpapers and china. But Japanese taste was not the only exotic influence that made the Victorian heart beat faster. Brasses and peacock feathers from India, fretwork screens and blue tiles from Morocco, Chinese porcelains, Arabic calligraphy, Venetian glass, Viennese bronze, all found places of honor in Victorian homes.

The Victorian Sensibility

Objects didn't have to come from faraway to be novel, of course. The Victorians also excelled at creating articles of their own invention for extremely specific purposes. There were pickle forks and croquette servers, hat-pin holders and glove stretchers, calling card receivers and spoon warmers. Many of the objects in this book fall into this category, and part of their charm is their very obsolescence. Who, after all, can resist a silver filigree posy holder?

In a way, it is just these small, over-specialized objects, created for long-gone purposes, that give us the best imaginative insight into the Victorian era. Certainly, many of these things were dreamed up by a nouveau riche society intent on flaunting its wealth and savoir faire. But when you actually pick up a skirt lifter, slip the ring onto your finger, and examine the clip, you can't help but think yourself back, even momentarily, in the Victorian world. How does the clip fasten to the skirt? Would you put it squarely in front of your feet, or a bit to the side, for a more attractive drape? Does it hold as well on silk as it does on serge?

Perhaps the strongest appeal of Victoriana for us is actually this sort of escapist fantasy. For once the century turned, and the aesthetics of modernism became predominant, fringe and braid and elaborate valances disappeared. Mahogany fell into complete disfavor. Chintz took on grandmotherly connotations. The word "hideous" was used to describe London's Albert Memorial. The peacock-feather vases and repoussé silver pitchers, the streaky majolica plates and animal-shaped inkwells were put away in attics. Where they have been waiting patiently ever since for us to discover and cherish them all over again.

The hall served a special purpose in the Victorian home. It was not exactly a room, yet it was a discrete space with its own important function. The hall was, essentially, a buffer zone between indoors and out, between the public world and the private. These distinctions were possibly more important a hundred years ago than we can readily appreciate today. In physical terms, a separate hall was a practical way to conserve heat and prevent cold drafts. In an era when central heating was still somewhat novel, excluding cold air was a seasonal concern. Streets, too, were often muddy and wet (or worse, since horses were still quite common on city streets until very late in the nineteenth century). The hall, therefore, provided a place to remove wet or dirty outer garments and to spruce up one's appearance in general.

The hall also provided a neutral, sheltered space for handling external matters. Most Victorian homes functioned without a telephone (which was invented in 1876). What's more, shoppers rarely carried home their own packages, but had them delivered. Mail came several times a day in urban areas, so even the middle-class Victorian hall was busy all day with messengers and callers. (In homes that employed servants, one of the first jobs that a housewife delegated was the task of answering the door.) In some ways, the hall could probably be likened to the reception area of a twentieth-century business.

And just as modern reception spaces are decorated to set a certain tone, so was the Victorian hall. Dignity was essential, since the most important visitors entered this way, but the space was basically utilitarian, and looked it.

The floor, for instance, was often tiled or covered with linoleum or another waterproof material. The walls were usually covered in a dark paper or paneled in dark wood, and were hung with inoffensive art. The furnishings were usually quite scanty. A pair of simple chairs, an umbrella stand, a hat rack, and a mirror were standard. Many homes featured a massive piece of furniture that combined several of these functions: a hall stand that comprised mirror, hooks for coats, and a broad seat (often hinged to create storage space). A small table, frequently displaying a card receiver in middle-class households, usually completed the furnishings in the hall. Although it was supposed to give an impression of respectability, the hall was always secondary, merely a prelude to the main public space in any Victorian house: the parlor.

"Dear Mrs. Mack,
My visiting-list is so large
that I never get round it once
in two years. I have solemnly
promised Mr. Mortimer
that I shall not know
another person."

MRS. M.E.W. SHERWOOD,
A Transplanted Rose, 1882

Front hall, Edward Lauterbach Residence, 1899
2 East 78th Street, New York City
Museum of the City of New York
The Byron Collection

STICK 'EM UP

Although there are records of antler chandeliers appearing as early as 1400, objects made from antlers look very Victorian today. This umbrella stand brought a whiff of the rugged outdoors into the front hall, suggesting long tramps on the moors. In England, where it was made, such associations would seem rather aristocratic since the prosperous middle class was predominantly urban while the nobility traditionally derived its wealth and power from immense rural land-holdings.

The walking sticks displayed here were an essential part of the nineteenth century gentleman's turnout. Canes and sticks became fashionable in the eighteenth century as civilian wearing of swords declined. In fact, many early sticks concealed weapons. By the mid-nineteenth century they were rarely used in self-defense; more often they provided self-definition. The elaborately carved heads of canes and sticks came in many materials: wood, bone, ivory, or precious metal. The shanks were usually made of wood, often ebonized, or bamboo.

A gentleman paying a call was expected to take his hat, gloves, and walking stick into the drawing room with him to indicate that he was staying for only a moment. But as one etiquette manual pointed out, this practice permitted him to hang onto his own property. "New umbrellas have been taken instead of old, as we all know," the manual notes, indicating that some things have not changed at all in a hundred years.

Antler umbrella stand, English, late 19th century;
Wood, ivory, and bone walking sticks, late 19th century
COLLECTION ANITA SAULINO WOLFSON

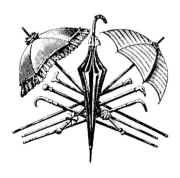

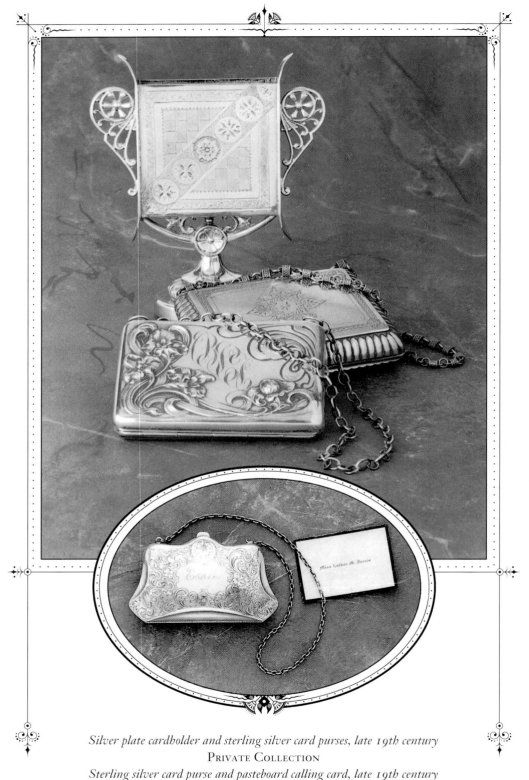

Silver plate cardholder and sterling silver card purses, late 19th century
PRIVATE COLLECTION
Sterling silver card purse and pasteboard calling card, late 19th century
PRIVATE COLLECTION

HOLDING ALL THE CARDS

The use of calling cards is said to have originated in seventeenth-century France, when gentlemen would write their name and address on the back of a playing card to give to a new acquaintance. If this story is true, they must have ruined many decks of cards. In any case, before long, it was common practice to have cards (still the size of a playing card) specially engraved with this information, and, as the century went on, with decorative birds, flowers, or other elaborate designs.

By the middle of the nineteenth century, cards had shrunk to the dimensions of today's business card (their modern descendant) and were used very heavily in middle- and upper-class social routines. The "call" was the basic social transaction for genteel Victorian women. It consisted of a ceremonial visit, ten or fifteen minutes long. The lady making the call did not even remove her hat or gloves; she merely perched on the edge of a chair with her purse on her lap and made small talk. Then, on her way out, she left her card.

Many ladies had small silver purses like the ones pictured here, and one etiquette book mentions that "Even so simple a thing as extracting a card from a card-case a novice sometimes finds difficult of accomplishment; the thin card eludes gloved fingers. . . ."

There would usually be an appropriate receptacle for cards on the front hall table, often a salver or a specially made cardholder like this one that displayed the number—and identity—of the hostess' visitors. The card shown in the inset photograph is edged in black to indicate that its owner, Miss Esther M. Ferris, was in mourning.

CALL WAITING

Though the ritual of paying calls was time-consuming, it provided a system for forming and maintaining friendships. "Knowing" someone, a hundred years ago, was a concept with considerable weight.

"Do you know Mrs. Sargent?" meant "do you exchange calls?" Every matron had what was called a "visiting list." On this list were the names of all members of her and her husband's families, and the long list of people who were her chosen friends. To keep the ties in this group current, it was necessary to call on everyone at least twice a year.

Of course, calls were made more often between closer friends. For instance, it was essential to pay a call in cases of illness, bereavement, or after one had been entertained by someone. New brides had to pay an extensive round of calls in recognition of their new social identities. And calls had to be returned; lack of reciprocity meant a resolution to discontinue the relationship.

The flowered box in the main photograph opens out to reveal a double row of wire clips. It may have been placed in the hall as a repository for visitors' calling cards. Or possibly, a very organized matron used it to file the cards of everyone on her visiting list, thus making it the Victorian equivalent of the Rolodex.

The plain wooden box in the inset photograph may have been used for mail or calling cards. Its presence in Mrs. Rigby's front hall or on her door didn't necessarily mean she was absent from the house. "Not at home" was, among Victorian matrons, a euphemism for "upstairs reading French novels," or "in the kitchen wrestling with a piecrust," or, simply, "doesn't want to see you."

Wooden box with celluloid panel and wire racks, late 19th century
COLLECTION JOYCE BALDWIN
Wooden mailbox, late 19th century
SOOKY GOODFRIEND II GALLERY

THE *Parlor*

*They say no sovereign was ever more loved
than I am (I am bold enough to say),
and this because of our domestic home,
the good example it presents.*

QUEEN VICTORIA, 1844

Drawing room, 1894
Museum of the City of New York
The Byron Collection
Background wallpaper design: Schumacher

The hall was a transitional place in the Victorian house, a space people passed through but didn't linger in. The parlor, on the other hand, presented the family's face to the world. It was the most public room, the place where guests were received, and where strangers would form their first impressions. The way the parlor looked, from the shade of paint on the walls to the music on the piano, from the pattern on the carpet to the books on the shelves, was significant.

Of course style presumes choice, and choice in home furnishings was a relatively new phenomenon in the Victorian era. Once prosperity reached the multitudes, the look of her parlor became as important to the Victorian woman as the style and trimming of her best church-going hat. To that end, the parlor was inevitably the best room in the house. The most attractive views, the highest ceilings, the largest fireplace, the biggest windows: all were allotted to the parlor. This tendency was so marked that in New York City, brownstones are said to have a "parlor floor," notable for possessing all the amenities; the upper floors were much less grand. Even the crudest houses on the frontier had one room set aside for "best."

In the first few decades of the Victorian era, the central item in any parlor was a table. It stood smack in the middle of room (often under a plaster rosette on the ceiling), covered with a heavy, decorative cloth. A lamp was placed at the center and the family gathered around this table to read, sew, write letters, or talk. Since kerosene lamps required a great deal of upkeep to shed a clean bright light, a household might use only one lamp after dark. The family circle, in these cases, was a literal term.

The basic furniture for a parlor was fundamentally similar to modern living room furniture. Although there were some extraordinary pieces produced in the era (the "S"-shaped sofa known as a tête-à-tête is one example), the vast majority of Victorian furniture might fit into the average current decorating scheme. A "parlor suite" offered by Sears at the end of the century consisted of a sofa, two arm chairs, and a pair of easy chairs, all upholstered in the customer's choice of corduroy, silk tapestry, or silk damask, and finished with fringe, cord, tassels, and fancy bindings.

The parlor furniture, though, however carefully chosen, was only part of the picture. The substantial seating pieces mentioned above were just the beginning. They would be joined, as soon as practicable, by further refinements: a piano or organ. Several smaller tables. Framed pictures, perhaps chromolithographs of Old Masters or hand-colored prints produced by Currier and Ives.

Wall and window treatments were also evidence of a homeowner's taste and pocketbook. The single-color walls of the earlier nineteenth century gave way to a more elaborate scheme. In the 1850s and '60s large-scaled *trompe l'oeil* wallpapers were fashionable: bouquets of roses tied with ribbon, oversized branches of fruit, trellises with scenic "views." Later in the century, William Morris's reforming views took hold and patterns became smaller, flatter, closer to abstract. But walls weren't necessarily quiet. The floor-to-ceiling spread was broken up, in the "Aesthetic style," into three areas: a frieze next to the ceiling, the "filling," down to roughly waist height, and below that, separated by a chair rail, the "dado." Each area was usually covered with a different pattern.

Adding to the mix were the various fabrics in the room. Suites of furniture were usually upholstered in the same fabric, often in a deep crimson that we identify readily with the period. But upholstery fabric was only the beginning. Long curtains called portieres shrouded doorways to help contain heat and ward off drafts. Fringed and swagged valances hung from mantels, and shawls draped pianos.

Windows were triply shrouded. Next to the glass as the first line of defense against the unwanted sunlight hung a layer of gauze or lace that was always drawn. Next came gathered curtains of a dark, heavy fabric that could be pulled across the window to block the invasive rays. Above it all loomed draped and pleated valances, often trimmed with braid and tassels. Privacy was a paramount concern. Many Victorian city-dwellers were living in closer proximity to strangers than they ever had before, and they made a great effort to prevent any hint of intrusion from the outside world.

It was a room well calculated to make complete idleness most easy. The tables were covered with a mass of albums, vases of flowers, and a quantity of entirely useless knick-knacks.

E.F. BENSON, *Dodo*, 1893

The finishing touch to the parlor decor was, of course, the knick-knacks for which the Victorian age is famous. No surface was left empty. There were boxes and saucers and potpourri bowls, figurines and albums and framed photographs. There were bead flowers and alabaster grapes and bouquets made out of feathers. Glass-sided boxes called "vitrines" exhibited collections of china or quartzes, while potted palms and rubber plants bristled in dark corners, reminders of faraway, hot, exotic climates.

And all of these things had some significance. A display case full of shells meant that someone had a scientific bent, and had spent hours stooping on a beach. Souvenirs of travel were really novel in those days: today's cliché of a teaspoon from Niagara Falls provided proud proof positive in the Victorian period that someone had actually made the trip, heard the thundering water, felt the spray on his or her face. Thus Victorian parlors were virtual museums of their inhabitants' experience or aspirations.

The Victorian home was widely thought of as a temple to domesticity, a pure and comfortable refuge from the crudeness and stress of the outside world. It was also the sole indicator of status for the middle class. All entertaining was done at home and many of the status indicators that we have come to rely on in the twentieth century—education, club affiliations, cars, designer clothes—did not exist. It was essential, then, that the parlor convey, in the words of Victorian decorating expert Mary Gay Humphreys, "a sense of elegance, good taste, recognition of the polite arts, and of graceful, social amenities."

HOUSEHOLD CRAFTS

They didn't have television. They didn't have radios. No movies. No comic books. What the Victorians did have to fill their time were long novels—and crafts. Every woman knew how to sew and knit, and those who didn't have to make or mend their menfolks' clothes turned their hands to more decorative tasks.

Embellishment was always popular. Mantels had fringed plush valances, pianos were draped in shawls. The floral arrangement on the mat of this family photograph is unusual, but entirely typical. The gold braid, pearlized paper chips, silk rosettes, and tiny embroidered flowers were probably purchased, while the dried flowers were no doubt gathered and dried at home. Like many Victorian crafts, this arrangement required a level of manual dexterity and skill (though not, perhaps, visual creativity) that seems remarkable today.

So does the beadwork on the tray. From the early nineteenth century, paper designs for stitchery (something like today's needlepoint canvases) were published in Berlin. Later, they were also made in London, and in time the embroidery was enlivened with, or worked entirely in, glass beads. This asymmetrical design, with its combination of Eastern geometric patterns and central motif of fairly naturalistic flowers, probably dates from the 1880s.

Photograph framed with real and artificial flowers, late 19th century
PROPOSITION RENTALS
Bead tray, English, c. 1880
YALE R. BURGE ANTIQUES

Two By Two

In the nineteenth century, nearly every parlor had a fireplace, and nearly every fireplace had a mantel. And every mantel that had any pretensions to gentility sported some kind of "ornament."

Nineteenth-century developments in molded ceramics made ceramic decorative accessories newly available to everyone. The English county of Staffordshire was the center of production for these figures, which first appeared in the 1840s. Sometimes called "flat backs" because many were not modeled in the round, they were turned out by very small factories and vary widely in quality. Some are quite slapdash. These examples, however, are fully modeled in quite excellent detail.

The most comical aspect of some Staffordshire figures was the careless adaptation of the molds. Particularly for figures of people, makers simply changed details or glazing, so that a mold might be used for both Gladstone and Disraeli (both prime ministers, but of opposing political parties). The first figure of Queen Victoria was made from a mold that had been used for an opera star; the manufacturer merely added a crown and changed the title.

Although people both historical and legendary were popular, animals had an even bigger public. Unless individual beasts were being portrayed (like the London Zoo's famous elephant, "Jumbo"), animals were always paired for symmetrical display. Poodles, pugs, greyhounds, and dalmatians were made, but spaniels were by far the most common. Both the dogs and the cats here show the characteristic red-brown glaze that appears on much Staffordshire ware, as well as traces of gilding to highlight the dogs' collars and the cats' bows.

Pair of ceramic cats, Staffordshire, England, late 19th century
HOFFMAN-GAMPETRO ANTIQUES
Pair of ceramic dogs, Staffordshire, England, late 19th century
HOFFMAN-GAMPETRO ANTIQUES

Berlin wool work fire screens, English, c. 1845
COLLECTION JAMES BEELAND ROGERS, JR.
Small leather bellows, late 19th centuy
COLLECTION CECILY BARTH FIRESTEIN

HEARTH AND HOME

The fireplace played a big part in the domestic arrangements of the parlor. Even after central heating was invented and families no longer depended solely on a fire for warmth, new houses featured a fireplace in the parlor, if nowhere else. As western society shifted into a more mobile, industrialized form, no one was willing to abandon the potent domestic symbol of the hearth.

These fire screens date from an earlier period, probably around 1845, when an open fire was indeed the only source of heat in a room. They would be placed on a table to shield a lady's face from the heat, lest her delicate complexion be reddened (or run: some makeup was based on wax). They are made of Berlin wool work, a Victorian precursor of needlepoint in which designs were embroidered on coarse canvas.

The bellows are a small, ladylike version of the tool that forced air onto the flames. If a fire went out or burned inadequately, rooms could be extremely cold, especially for women dressed in décolletage for the evening. One American woman who married an Englishman at the turn of the century refused most winter dinner invitations at country houses because she couldn't stand shivering for hours in her low-cut gowns.

THE LADY AND THE LAMP

When we think back to the inconveniences of the Victorian era, we tend to focus on the lack of plumbing, but in fact the lack of what we think of as sufficient light had an even greater effect on daily life. The supremacy of the kerosene lamp dictated much of a family's interaction after dark. Kerosene lamps required a lot of work. They had to be filled daily, their wicks had to be trimmed, the chimneys and shades had to be washed often because they became blackened by smoke. It was common practice for a family of modest means to light only one lamp at nightfall, and to gather around it at a parlor table with books or crafts or games.

The advent of gas and electricity in the 1880s and '90s broke up the circle around the table. Suddenly there were strong light sources around the perimeter of the room, because gas or electric lights were fixed to the walls.

Then, as now, lamps were considered decorative as well as functional objects. This gas lamp, which bears an 1816 date, was originally a graceful neoclassical statue. To modern eyes, its later conversion into a lamp is not completely felicitous: the large glass chimney and brass-trimmed workings contrast sharply with the statue's delicate draperies. But this kind of adaptation would have been considered very "artistic" one hundred years ago.

Gas lamp, English, late 19th century
COLLECTION JAMES BEELAND ROGERS, JR.

Pair of glass vases, Bohemian, c. 1865
COLLECTION CORNELIUS BOUSIE

BOHEMIAN STYLE

Bohemian glassware (produced in a region of what is now the Czech Republic) was exhibited at London's Great Exhibition in 1851, where visitors were charmed by two novel characteristics: its colors (most English glass up to this date was clear) and the delicate engraving used to decorate it. Imports increased as a direct result of the Exhibition, and many pieces like these appeared in English and American parlors over the next twenty-five years.

These vases exhibit many of the typical characteristics of Bohemian glass. First is the amber color, which, along with ruby, was commonly used. The delicately engraved rose garlands are classic Bohemian ornament, as is the heavy shape. Finally, the panel-cut stems and the star-shaped cutting on the underside of the square feet are also characteristic.

Bohemian glass was widely successful partly because, until mid-century, decorative glass was very expensive. In England there were government limits on manufacturing (repealed in 1845), and until press-molding was invented in 1827, all glass had been hand-blown and cut. Bohemian glass was therefore a new and relatively inexpensive version of what had until very recently been a luxury item.

JUST FOR SHOW

Every parlor with pretensions to middle-class standing had some surface devoted to displaying what the Victorians called "ornaments." It might be nothing more than a pine whatnot covered with colored paper, but the ability to consecrate space (to say nothing of capital) to the purely decorative was an important and symbolic leap into the bourgeoisie.

The Bohemian glass vases, opposite, are artifacts from the middle of the century, while the vases on this page probably date from the 1880s. Their square toothlike feet show a strong Japanese influence, as do some of the flowers and insects painted on their surfaces.

The goblet is a nineteenth-century revival of an eighteenth-century design. It was made on Murano, a small island in the Venetian lagoon where elaborate hand-blown glass has been produced for centuries. The strong turquoise of the dolphins and the crimped rim of the goblet (which would seem to exempt it from practical use) were especially popular in the 1880s and '90s.

What all of these objects have in common is that they imply a high level of sophistication. Although they may have been displayed on an American mantel, they brought a whiff of the exotic into the domestic world.

Glass cylinder vases with enameled decorations, English, c. 1880
KENTSHIRE GALLERIES
Glass goblet, Venetian, probably before 1900
BARR-GARDNER ASSOCIATES, LTD.

Shardware plate, late 19th century
COLLECTION JAMES BEELAND ROGERS, JR.

SHATTERPROOF

China breaks. It's a fact of life. And in the days before Krazy Glue, it was hard to put the pieces back together again. This shardware plate is an example of a classic Victorian response to breakage.

Shardware was to china what patchwork quilts were to worn-out clothes: recycling. This plate is an unusually forceful example, with the two halves of the teacup jutting out into space. Although most of the scraps are blue, they do not all come from the same set of china. There are bits of the rust color that was used on Imari pieces (see pages 72 and 80), as well as patterns in a different shade of blue. The artisan must have collected shards from various household accidents and pieced them together carefully to cover as much of the surface as possible. The neat edging of shells (mostly clamshells) gives the ensemble a vaguely briny, nautical note.

Creating shardware killed several Victorian birds with one stone. It was thrifty (reusing of broken china), it involved collecting (assembling the right size shells and pieces of china), and it was the kind of hobby that could fill long evenings. And the end result made a splendid conversation piece: if chat lagged, the hostess could regale guests with the pedigree of every fragment she had used.

THE POTTER'S ART

By the latter part of the nineteenth century, the return to handicrafts urged by Charles Eastlake and William Morris had inspired a wave of "art manufacture." Department stores were full of "art furniture," "art glass," and "art pottery," articles that were carefully crafted and often decorated by hand.

After the 1876 Philadelphia Centennial Exposition, American potters began experimenting with underglaze decoration like that seen on the European pottery displayed at the exhibition. These pieces are all in the "Louwelsa" pattern, made by the Weller pottery in Zanesville, Ohio, after 1893. (Only the two center pieces are marked, but the two unmarked pieces are stylistically identical to them.)

Louwelsa pottery featured hand-painted fruits or flowers, or sometimes Indian portraits, on brown-glazed pottery in simple shapes. The glazing technique was adapted from one used by the more illustrious Rookwood pottery in Cincinnati, which was more expensive than Louwelsa. This was art pottery—which signaled sophistication and refined taste—for the multitudes.

Earthenware vessels, two marked "Louwelsa,"
Samuel Weller, Zanesville, Ohio, 1893-1930
PRIVATE COLLECTION

Flower-patterned celluloid-covered
photograph album, late 19th century
PRIVATE COLLECTION
Celluloid-covered photograph album and
celluloid-covered autograph album, American, c. 1890
ACCENTS UNLIMITED, LTD.

THE FAMILY ALBUM

As the Victorians collected chromolithographs and stamps and fossils and souvenirs, they also collected people. Commercial photography began to flourish in the 1860s, and photographs maintained considerable novelty value through the era. Pictures of friends or family were displayed with pride in handsome albums. Very old family albums (dating from mid-century) often display blurry or poorly composed pictures that would be discarded today, but a hundred years ago even an out-of-focus portrait was worth preserving.

Many albums featured pages that were die-cut for standard-sized photographs. One of the most popular sizes was called "carte de visite." These 2 ½ x 3 ½ inch cardboard-mounted photographs were relatively inexpensive and were a popular format to exchange among friends, the way we exchange wallet-sized snapshots today. They were also issued in sets that depicted famous people—royalty, actors, even famous preachers. (Here the analogy might be baseball cards.)

The smallest album pictured here was for autographs, another popular Victorian way of collecting people that has survived to this day.

IN LIVING COLOR

Throughout the Victorian period, technology had an enormous influence over aesthetics. These three albums are filled with a characteristic product of the last quarter of the nineteenth century: chromolithographs, often known as "chromos." They were created by the old printmaking technique of lithography, which uses inked stones instead of metal plates to carry the image. But chromolithographs, as the pseudo-Greek name implies, used color. Several stones were inked in different shades, and when they were printed in the correct order, the result came out in natural-looking hues.

Chromolithography was immensely popular. It permitted modest households to have brightly colored pictures on their walls (often reproductions of famous oil paintings). Chromolithographed valentines, Christmas cards, and postcards (invented in 1873) swelled the mails.

One of the most popular uses for chromolithography was the trade card. These were handed out by salesmen, given away as premiums, displayed in stores, and collected by families. The two larger albums here are full of trade cards advertising items ranging from thread to flour to tobacco, all collected by a Vermont family in the early 1880s.

The smaller album holds chromolithographed calling cards. These are elaborate versions of the cards usually used (see pages 16-17) to substitute for a personal visit. The very popular hand motif suggests the sentimental Victorian ideal of personal contact, co-opted in our day by advertising for telephone services.

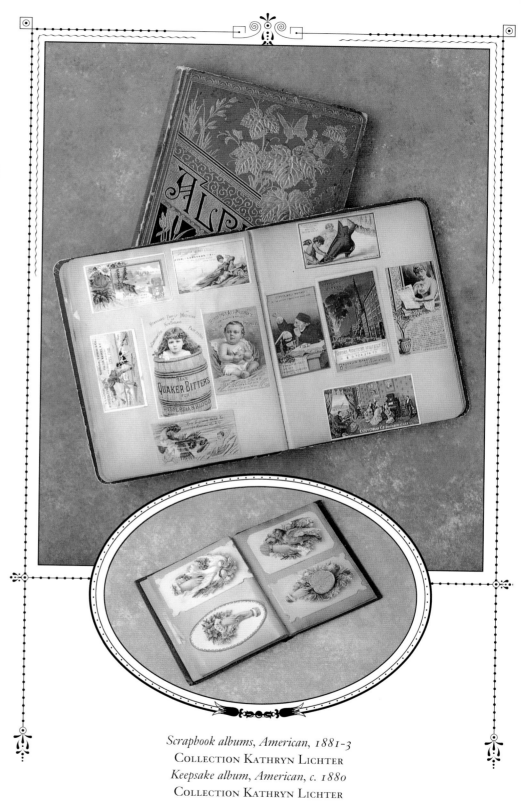

Scrapbook albums, American, 1881-3
COLLECTION KATHRYN LICHTER
Keepsake album, American, c. 1880
COLLECTION KATHRYN LICHTER

Beaded pillows, late 19th century
COLLECTION CECILY BARTH FIRESTEIN
Sailor's whimsy, English, late 19th century
LAURA FISHER

PILLOW TALK

Until 1845, glass in England was a very expensive commodity. But when an excise tax on glass was repealed in that year, crafts using glass beads (as well as other glasswork such as the Kilner weights on page 44) became much more widespread. Throughout the Victorian era, craft shops distributed the materials and patterns for many hobbies such as Berlin wool work (see the fire shields on page 24) and shell boxes (see page 136).

Purple cushions with clear glass beads are quite common in antique stores today, so it seems probable that this was a very popular color combination among genteel ladies. On the other hand, some dealers attribute these purple pillows with clear beadwork to Native Americans of the northeastern United States. Many relics of the Victorian era, like these, are virtually undocumented and have so far resisted exact identification.

Sailor's whimsies are another little-studied form of folk art. They are sometimes called "sailor's valentines," a term that seems to cover any crafts combining nautical motifs and heart shapes. This little pillow, elaborately beaded and embroidered, bears the insignia of the Devonshire Regiment and two sentimental poems. The assumption is that sailor's whimsies, like scrimshaw, were created by sailors on long ocean voyages, which provided a lot of time for brooding about their sweethearts back home.

WHIMS AND FANCIES

Although many of the crafts practiced a hundred years ago have died out (nobody works with hair anymore, for instance), this whimsy in a bottle is an example of a craft that is still current, if unusual. It is related to the building of ships in bottles, though whimsies come in many different forms. This one, dated 1884, may be a kind of Christmas tree. Circuses were also made, and crucifixes with all the symbols of the Passion (nails, a spear) are fairly common.

This is a craft that does not require a great deal in terms of materials: this whimsy is made of wood, silk thread, and tiny metal rings; the containers were often recycled liquor or vinegar bottles. But great skill is necessary to whittle the wood and, above all, to erect the construction within the tiny confines of the bottle. This example has a stopper that can't be removed, which seems a sound final precaution.

Glass, wood, silk thread, and metal whimsy in a bottle, 1884
LYME REGIS, LTD.

Bronze elephant statues, Japanese, late 19th century
BARR-GARDNER ASSOCIATES, LTD.

CALL OF THE WILD

One overwhelmingly common theme in Victorian decorative arts is animals. In this book alone there are pitchers shaped like fish, an inkwell shaped like a crab, an eagle-shaped nutcracker, and bats on a pin tray. The Victorians were fascinated with the natural world (if fauna dominated decorative accessories, think of the flora on the walls, floors, and furniture). They were especially excited by its more exotic members, like elephants.

Pachyderms had a lot to recommend them. Their amazingly flexible trunks, their vast size, and their generally peaceable temperaments made them appealing (the faint but definite threat implicit in their size added a pleasant frisson of danger). They came from very far away. Rajahs rode on them.

In 1865 the London Zoo bought an elephant named Jumbo from the Jardin des Plantes in Paris. Seventeen years later (after some highly public controversy that spawned several popular songs) the zoo sold Jumbo to P.T. Barnum for $10,000. On the way to the ship that would take him to America, Jumbo staged a sit-in, refusing to move from his spot in the street. More public interest, more fame for elephants, all gravy to Mr. Barnum. Even Jumbo's death was newsworthy: he charged a railway train in Canada. (A fatal mistake.)

These bronze statues were made in Japan for export to the elephant-mad West, probably late in the nineteenth century when European and American markets were eager for novel Japanese goods.

IVORY TRADE

A display of ivory curios like these served several purposes. On the simplest level, it occupied space. This was an era that abhorred a vacuum, and all advisors on design took for granted that flat spaces would be adorned with ornaments, even of the meanest, most ordinary nature—which these elegantly carved and engraved items certainly are not.

Second, these exotic ornaments provided something to talk about. This was no mean service considering how many topics were taboo a hundred years ago (sex, money, politics, religion). When conversation languished, the eager visitor could always ask his hostess just what those creatures marching on the elephant tusk were.

Finally, objects like these lent their owner distinction. It took a modicum of sophistication even to know that such articles existed, and where they might be bought. If they had been purchased in some back-street bazaar in Poona or Madras, so much the better. The cost was probably less relevant than the connoisseurship or experience implied in their presence on a parlor table.

Carved ivory boxes, picture frame, and figurines, possibly Japanese, late 19th century
COLLECTION JUDY SINGER
Carved elephant tusk, possibly Indian, late 19th century
COLLECTION JUDY SINGER

Oh Christmas Tree

The Christmas tradition of bringing pine trees indoors and decorating them was brought to England from the Continent around the middle of the nineteenth century. In 1848, pictures of Queen Victoria and Prince Albert's gaily decked Christmas tree appeared in illustrated newspapers worldwide. Royal customs spread quickly, and by the latter half of the nineteenth century, many families in Britain and America had amassed collections of ornaments like these to hang on their own trees. Gifts, usually for the children, were also suspended from the tree's branches.

The delicate glass ornaments in the main photograph do not look very different from ornaments that are still made today, although the fur-clad young lady on the swing does have a certain Victorian demureness. Our conception of Santa Claus has not changed at all in a hundred years. Any small child would recognize this one.

The paper ornaments in the inset photograph are known as "Dresdens," for the town in Germany where they were traditionally made. These highly detailed decorations are made from two identical pieces of pressed cardboard glued together to create a realistic three-dimensional object. They came in many fanciful shapes, including musical instruments, vehicles, animals, and food.

Glass, wire, and cotton batting Christmas ornaments,
probably German, late 19th century
COLLECTION JOYCE BALDWIN
Cardboard Christmas ornaments, German, late 19th century
COLLECTION JOYCE BALDWIN

PARLOR GAMES

Although twentieth-century families rarely sit in their living rooms singing songs or gluing shells to boxes, we do still play what the Victorians thought of as parlor games. They did not often play cards because card games usually involved gambling, which was considered immoral. But they played word games, board games, dominoes (a very old game imported from Europe), and, especially popular from about 1890 to 1900, table croquet.

Table croquet was a natural offshoot of the game played on the lawn, but miniaturized. These mallets are only twelve inches high. The court was set up on a table top, with the ribbon strap clamped vertically to the table edges to provide a boundary.

Table croquet could be played by both children and adults and, like its outdoor progenitor, allowed the sexes to compete on an equal basis. This was doubtless one factor in the enormous popularity of outdoor croquet.

Although its origins are cloudy, the game was introduced in England in the 1850s and in America in the 1860s. It was one of the few ways that corseted, hoop-skirted women could get physical exercise, but they had to hit the ball one-handed, using the other hand to hold their skirts out of the way.

The new popularity of the rotary lawn mower in the 1880s probably prolonged the fashionable life of croquet. The closely clipped lawn necessary for the game was more easily maintained by a lawn mower than by the previous method of tedious, labor-intensive scything. Croquet eventually yielded to the more strenuous lawn tennis, whose indoor tabletop version, table tennis, is a bit too lively for the parlor.

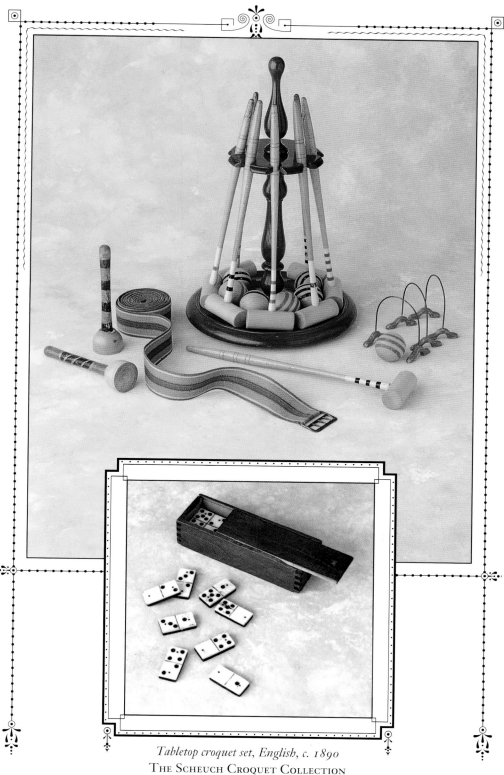

Tabletop croquet set, English, c. 1890
THE SCHEUCH CROQUET COLLECTION
Horn dominoes in wooden box, English, late 19th century
MAN-TIQUES LTD.

Rosewood, ebony, silver, and ivory zither,
Karl Kirchner, Vienna, 1878
E. BUK

THE SOUND OF MUSIC

Making music was another common family pursuit in the Victorian era. One of the standard badges of middle-class rank was the possession of a piano or parlor organ, and every young lady or aspirant to ladyhood learned how to play. Although what we think of as classical music was often performed, a pianist would be just as likely to accompany a singer. Music publishing was a big business, and popular songs like Sir Arthur Sullivan's "The Lost Chord" were published in several different keys to accommodate every vocal range.

The possibilities for flirtation were extensive. A gentleman might turn the pages of a lady's music. If he had a pleasant voice, he might offer to sing a ballad, conditional on a favored lady's accompanying him. Piano duets were sometimes arranged to include crossing parts, forcing one player to reach over the other player's hands to reach his or her notes.

Other smaller instruments were also common in Victorian parlors. The zither pictured here was made in Vienna. It was clearly intended for an upper-class musician, since its materials (rosewood, ebony, silver, and ivory) are quite luxurious.

The zither is a difficult instrument to play. Chords are plucked on the five fretted strings while the pegged strings are strummed or plucked with the other hand. A hundred years ago it was probably played as accompaniment to lieder or traditional songs, though instrumental pieces such as waltzes were written for it. The zither wasn't a gender-specific instrument, but frequent playing would produce calluses on the fingers, never desirable for the Victorian lady.

Pan The Piper

The Western visual arts go through cycles of neoclassicism, and after the glory years of the "picturesque," promoted by Eastlake, Morris, and the Aesthetic movement, designers returned to the Greeks and Romans for inspiration. The occasionally fevered ornament and clutter yielded to a more "chaste" and "suitable" look. Jacobean was out; Palladian was in.

This little Pan owes his existence to the late-nineteenth-century resurgence of neoclassicism. Pan, in Greek mythology, was a god of pastures and woodlands who played on the syrinx, a seven-reed pipe. In legend, he induced the sudden, contagious fear that led the Persians to abandon their attack on Greek soldiers at the battle of Marathon, hence our word "panic."

The unknown sculptor has taken a few liberties here: Pan is usually represented with the legs, tail, and horns of a goat, as well as a beard. This is a youthful and rather romantic Pan, slender and smooth-skinned, with only a tuft of vestigial tail. His pipes, rather than the traditional syrinx, are merely two long belled horns, but their length beautifully balances Pan's precarious tiptoe pose.

Bronze Pan statue, Italian, late 19th century
COLLECTION CORNELIUS BOUSIE

Earthenware wall plaques, Staffordshire, England, c. 1840
KENTSHIRE GALLERIES

FAITH OF THEIR FATHERS

Visually, these Staffordshire wall plaques are very typical of the 1840s. The pink and copper luster glaze, the discreet wreath and angel motif, and the simple leaf decorations in the corners are classic early Victorian.

So are the messages: "Praise Ye the Lord" and "Thou God, See'st Me." On both plaques the tiny writing at the top of the wreath proclaims: "In thee O Lord do I put my trust; let me never be confounded." (The quotation is from Psalm 31.)

It was a very religious era, and religion, in America and Europe alike, was predominantly Christian. Weekly attendance at church services was a foregone conclusion for a respectable family, and often families returned to church on Sunday afternoons for another dose of scripture and sermon. Large households, especially in England, held daily prayers for family and servants alike (usually before breakfast in the dining room—everyone knelt on the floor with their elbows on the dining room chairs). The family Bible was well-worn; children were expected to identify quotations, chapter and verse. In fact, some families read only scripture and played only with Biblical toys on Sundays. (Noah's ark was a favorite.) In a time when life expectancy was still quite short, the daily assurance that God was paying attention provided considerable comfort.

MIXED MEDIA

The Victorians used some improbable media to fashion decorative objects. The shell boxes (page 136) and the shardware plate (page 28) represent two of the more durable crafts that seem fairly appealing to moderns. People still decorate boxes with shells. They do not, however, create three-dimensional pictures out of hair. In fact, many people today are quite squeamish about one of the most popular Victorian crafts.

Hair, although part of the human body, does not deteriorate the way flesh does. This was one of the reasons it appealed to Victorians: as *Godey's Lady's Book* pointed out in 1860, "Hair is at once the most delicate and lasting of our materials and survives us like love." It was natural enough, given this attitude, that some jewelry made of hair (like the bow brooches on page 151) was intended as a memorial to a loved one. But hair crafts took other forms as well. This large (nineteen inches wide) and extremely elaborate wreath, worked in several colors of hair and decorated with china flowers, may have been simply a home craft project or a commemorative piece using family members' hair.

Hair work was very exacting. A book published in 1867 called *Self-Instructor in the Art of Hair Work* shows a man seated in front of a tiny round table that is covered with bobbins like those used for making lace. Directions for the "Square Chair Braid" begin "Take sixteen strands, eighty hairs in a strand. . . ." Little wonder that the craft has not survived!

Hair wreath with china flowers, late 19th century
PRIVATE COLLECTION

Painted bronze cat miniatures, probably Vienna, late 19th century
COLLECTION JUDY SINGER
Hand-painted terra-cotta bull mastiff and spaniel,
Bronze St. Bernard puppy inkwell (center), Vienna, all late 19th century
HOFFMAN-GAMPETRO ANTIQUES

COLLECTOR'S CHOICE

"Ours is a collecting age," proclaimed a British journal in 1869, and this sweeping generalization was widely and astutely accurate. The Victorians were great amassers of things, but they also loved systems and order. They liked to quantify and sort, to pinpoint similarities and differences, and they enjoyed the possibility of mastering a category. One striking example of this organizing urge is that in 1863, only twenty-two years after the invention of the postage stamp, a book called *The Stamp Collector's Guide* was published.

Collecting stamps was generally thought of as a boys' pursuit (along with collecting coins or birds' eggs) but collecting figures of dogs and cats seems likely to have been a feminine hobby.

The dogs in the lower picture are almost real-life puppy-size. The spaniel and the bull mastiff were crafted in hand-painted terra-cotta, while the St. Bernard puppy is a painted bronze inkwell: his head lifts up to reveal the ink bottle. Interest in dog breeds had flourished since the 1840s when the first single-breed dog shows were held in England, and these figures clearly exhibit with great orthodoxy the specific characteristics of their breeds.

The cat figurines are a different story. Painted, anthropomorphized miniatures like the ones pictured here were widely manufactured in Vienna for export and belong to the large category known logically enough as "Vienna bronzes." (The St. Bernard is also a Vienna bronze.) Some of these cats carry musical instruments, while the two rakish fellows who look like Puss in Boots are armed with rifles.

BIRD IN A GILDED CAGE

Denizens of the modern era who long for a little fantastic detail in their dwellings might envy the birds who lived in this cage. No article was too humble to deserve decoration in the Victorian era, and this domed cage (which was originally painted cream and blue) has a vaguely Anglo-Oriental air. The gallery on its tray and the rectangular framework of the cage are decorated with a pierced pattern reminiscent of "Chinese Chippendale" furniture. The bottom of the cage, visible when the cage is hanging, is decorated with a pink rose.

Then as now, birds were very common pets, and for much the same reasons. They are decorative and lively, but require little maintenance. They were obviously housed well. The paint on this cage, however, is lead-based, and since birds do tend to pick at things with their beaks, it might not have been the healthiest environment. One also wonders if the Victorians used humble newspaper for cage lining—or something altogether more decorative?

Painted wire bird cage, late 19th century
COLLECTION JUDY SINGER

Green glass weights, probably Kilner, English, 1850-1900
COLLECTION ANITA SAULINO WOLFSON

WEIGHTY MATTERS

Doorstops were unnecessary until the 1775 invention of a new hinge that caused doors to swing closed automatically. Since it wasn't always convenient to keep some doors closed (the kitchen door, for instance, sees a lot of traffic), doorstops began appearing. They were improvised at first out of earthenware and later made of cast bronze or brass, often with long handles so they could be moved more easily.

These green glass weights were probably made in the Kilner glass factory outside Wakefield, a small town in Yorkshire, England. They were sometimes called "dumpies" or "dumps" because they were made from leftover molten glass that would otherwise have been dumped at the end of the day. (The Kilner factory primarily made bottles.)

Kilner weights range from paperweights to massive ovals a foot high and weighing ten pounds. They often feature a potful of flowers that seems to be made of bubbles. In fact, the flowers in the pot were formed first, then cooled and possibly touched with chalk or a chemical. When the blooms were coated with fresh molten glass to create the weight, tiny air bubbles formed along their surfaces. Other, less common, motifs found in Kilner weights are cherubs, portrait busts, and commemorative themes. They were very common in the north of England and were sometimes used to line garden paths, or, with holes drilled in them, as doorknobs or finials for bedposts.

BEAUTY TO BURN

The brilliant Scottish designer Christopher Dresser certainly produced ingenious tableware in silver and glass (see pages 84 and 85). But he also produced designs for almost everything in the home, right down to objects as utilitarian as the coal scuttle. Many fireplaces, particularly in urban houses, burned coal rather than wood. Fuel reserves were hauled up from the coal cellar and deposited in receptacles next to each fireplace.

This coal scuttle was manufactured by a metalworking company called Benham & Froud. Dresser is known to have designed several earlier examples for the firm in the 1870s and '80s, though the boxy shapes of his other bins have little in common with the gleaming rotundity of this brass acorn. Although this design (from 1892) is not known absolutely to be Dresser's, its manufacturer's registration number falls between those of two documented Dresser designs.

The piece bears many of the hallmarks of Dresser's work. One is the flowing line of the wrought iron tripod and handle. (Until Dresser got hold of it, wrought iron had been used mainly for outdoor purposes like gates and lampposts.) In his designs toward the end of the century, he spun wrought iron into shapes that resemble Jack's enormous beanstalk, with a sinuous life of their own.

Also typical of Dresser are the exposed rivets and screws visible on the wrought iron frame. Like Eastlake and Morris, Dresser believed that the construction of objects should be explicitly obvious.

Brass and wrought iron coal scuttle and shovel attributed to Christopher Dresser, Benham & Froud, English, 1892
KURLAND · ZABAR GALLERY

Stereopticon and views, American, 1874
MAN-TIQUES LTD.

HOME ENTERTAINMENT

This unlikely looking object is the VCR of a hundred years ago. It is called a stereopticon, or a stereoscope. In this case, "stereo" referred to the two side-by-side photographs mounted on a card that the viewer slid into a rack. When they were looked at through the eyepiece, they merged into a three-dimensional image.

Stereopticons were standard equipment in the middle-class home. Millions were sold between the 1850s and World War I, and manufacturers like Underwood and Underwood also produced millions of cards, or "stereographs." Families collected them, often by theme, and compared or shared their collections with their friends. In the middle of the century landscapes were popular, especially the majestic scenery of the American wilderness. As photography progressed and photographs of people were easier to take, celebrities began appearing on stereographs. So did news events, like World's Fairs and the building of the Panama Canal.

Possessing a stereopticon and the latest sets of cards satisfied the Victorian passion for collecting and classifying. It was also an important badge of middle-class sophistication and affluence.

Photographic Memory

Until the development of photography, there was only one way to possess the image of a loved one: an artist had to execute a portrait. Even in the hands of the most competent professional, a likeness was subject to interpretation. Portraits, moreover, were costly.

The camera not only brought portraits within the means of the middle class, it also provided a new level of naturalistic detail and photography was embraced enthusiastically from the first. Even in the 1850s and '60's, when sitters had to be restrained with metal clamps for the long duration of the exposure and developing the glass plates involved potent chemicals, photography was a commercial success. Between 1851 and 1861, the number of photographers in England increased from 51 to 2,534. As the century went on, technical developments shortened the exposures, simplified developing, and replaced the glass plates with film. Even after George Eastman's introduction, in 1888, of the Kodak camera for the amateur, commercial portrait photographers thrived.

Exchanging photographs with friends and relatives was a popular pastime. By the last quarter of the century, clusters of silver-framed photographs were a standard decorative display on the occasional tables and piano lids of the well-to-do.

Shoe boxes full of unwanted snapshots were far in the future, though the stand for the brocade photo album in the inset photograph does contain an extra drawer for storage.

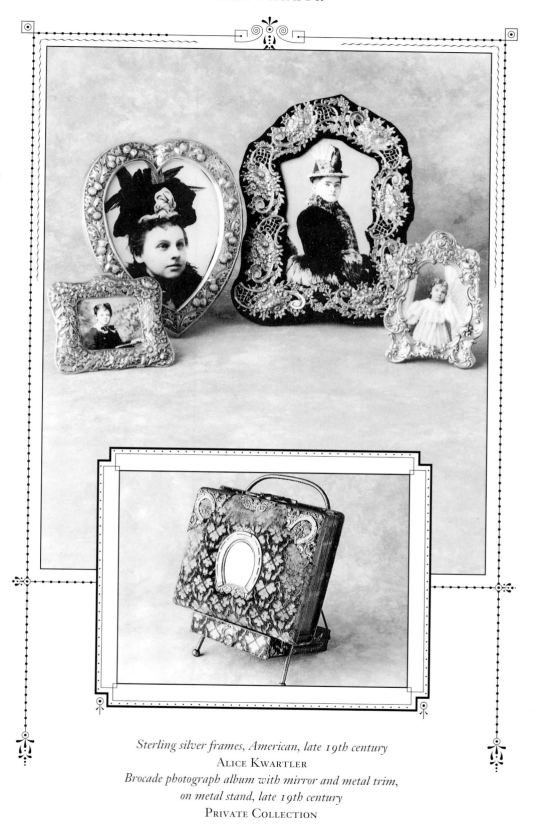

Sterling silver frames, American, late 19th century
ALICE KWARTLER
Brocade photograph album with mirror and metal trim,
on metal stand, late 19th century
PRIVATE COLLECTION

THE *Library*

The library was lined with books, and there were pictures
and statues, and distracting little cabinets full of
coins and curiosities, and Sleepy Hollow chairs, and
queer tables, and bronzes, and, best of all,
a great open fireplace with quaint tiles all around it.

LOUISA MAY ALCOTT, *Little Women*, 1868

Library, Chauncey Depew Residence, 1899
27 West 54th Street, New York City
Museum of the City of New York
The Byron Collection
Background wallpaper design: Schumacher

*I*f the parlor was the feminine center of the Victorian house, the library (or den, or smoking room) was emphatically the domain of the Victorian gentleman. More than his domain, it was his refuge.

The distinction between men's and women's spheres has seldom been as strong as it was in the Victorian era. Middle-class men went out daily into the fray of commerce, which was popularly imagined in the fiercest of terms. Leonard Jerome, a New York stockbroker in the 1870s and '80s, declared that Wall Street was "a jungle where men tear and claw." Ladies, meanwhile, shielded from the fierce conflicts that produced the almighty dollar, created a chaste and pleasant home where meals were prompt, linens smelled sweet, and children brought Papa his slippers.

But what if the chaste, pleasant atmosphere became a little bit . . . restrictive? After all, even the most proper paterfamilias must cut loose sometimes. Men will be men. It was widely accepted that men had a baser nature than women, and that they liked to participate, from time to time, in activities that women just wouldn't enjoy. Like smoking, for instance. Drinking. Talking about money and politics.

There were many Victorian venues for this kind of masculine diversion. Some of the fraternal organizations such as the Elks that still flourish today had their roots in this era. The urban men's clubs on the English model provided men with a womanless haven. And some men, who were wealthy enough to live in large houses, had their own little clubhouse at home in the form of a library.

The walls should be hung

with rich colors—

not so dark as to make it difficult

to light the room sufficiently

in the evening, but it must not be

too light, or we shall lose the

feeling of repose we most want.

RICHARD A. WELLS,
Manners Culture and Dress
of the American Best Society, 1890

Reading is to the mind what eating is to the body; and reflection is similar to digestion.

RICHARD A. WELLS,
Manners Culture and Dress of the American Best Society, 1890

This room was usually on the ground floor, along with the other reception rooms, but it was often tucked aside because it was likely that men would smoke in the library, and the fumes must not pollute the rest of the house.

The decorative scheme was much more sober than that of the parlor. The walls were usually covered with a richly colored paper or even paneled in dark wood. Bookshelves were often a feature, heavily built with architectural motifs such as arches, cornices, and gables. Furniture was also on the ponderous side, often Gothic or Elizabethan revival (they were thought to be "earnest" styles). In addition to a writing table or desk, the room usually contained a few extremely comfortable chairs upholstered in leather, which looked appropriately masculine and didn't harbor odors the way some fabrics might. The usual Victorian assortment of occasional tables filled in any empty corners.

Even the pictures hanging on the walls carried out the manly theme. No baskets of flowers or sentimental subjects here; in the library hung hunting pictures, such as engravings of Landseer's *The Stag at Bay* or bold landscapes, such as Frederick Church's florid mountain scenes. There might even be, depending on the level of wifely tolerance, pictures of a very faintly racy nature.

It was in the library, too, that the Victorian gentleman indulged his special interests. These might simply involve reading. A hundred years ago, women's education generally halted years before that of men, so it was not unusual for a man to have intellectual interests that outstripped those of his wife. (She was, in any case, not expected to read anything much more demanding than respectable fiction or household advice.) Science and history, too, were amateur pursuits for many men. A specimen case with carefully collected fossils or arrowheads or coins might occupy a prominent place.

Even if a man had no hobbies or collections, the library would sport its own form of Victorian clutter. As American writer Gervase Wheeler put it, this room should be "the magnetic gathering place of a thousand tasteful trifles—relics, specimens, objects of art, curiosities, suggestive nothings—which serve to make talk independent of politics, dress, fashion, and scandal." This is probably an overly fastidious point of view. Politics were theoretically out of bounds in polite company because political discussion so often created dissension, but among good friends, what (besides business) could be so interesting? Dress, fashion, and scandal, of course, were better left to the women, perched on their chintz sofas in the parlor.

Cloisonné enameled brass desk set, French, c. 1870
ACCENTS UNLIMITED, LTD.
Brass-cornered blotter and brass desk accessories, English, late 19th century
ANTIQUE CACHE

PEN AND INK

One field that has made great technical strides in the last hundred years is writing. Although typewriters were patented as early as the 1850s, it was years before these machines were common even in offices. All correspondence was written by hand. Written, moreover, with pens that had to be constantly dipped into inkwells, though Lewis Waterman's 1884 invention of a practical fountain pen with an ink reservoir put dipped pens out of business.

This handsome cloisonné desk set, and the brass accessories in the inset picture, hint at what a business writing was. The pagoda is actually an inkwell, as is the brass crab. (Novelty inkwells were very popular.) Letter openers slit open not only envelopes, but also the pages of books left uncut by printers. The rectangular blocks with knobs are blotters that were rolled over a written page to pick up excess ink.

The large flat blotters were covered with sheets of absorbent paper, and writers pressed their letters against this paper to hasten the drying process. (Servants were supposed to change blotting paper daily in grand houses and were reputed to read any traces of correspondence they could find.) The brown-bristled brush was used to clean pen points. This was all very elaborate, but a great deal more beautiful than a ballpoint pen or a floppy disk.

Cloisonné enamel was revived in France by a metalworker named Antoine Tard in the 1860s. His near-Eastern inspired cloisonné teapot, coffeepot, sugar bowl, and plate produced for the eminent silversmiths Christofle and Company were displayed at the Paris Exhibition of 1867, and may have influenced the exotic design of this desk set.

WRITING STYLE

Although carefully fitted boxes for sewing, writing, and toilet articles were common in the Victorian era, it is unusual for one to have survived in such pristine perfection as this writing compendium. As a mounted plaque announces, it was given to "Samuel G. Asher on the occasion of his confirmation with Leopold de Rothschild's best wishes." The date was 19 March 1881.

Samuel Asher was probably confirmed at the age of twelve or thirteen, and no doubt Mr. Rothschild assumed he looked forward to a lifetime of letter-writing. But since the contents of this writing case are untouched, we are left to wonder if the recipient perhaps had still another compendium he preferred.

In addition to a leather-bound tablet of paper and several sizes of stationery and envelopes, the case contains numerous ivory instruments: pens, a ruler, a penknife, a scraper (the only way to erase mistakes), scissors, an ink bottle, and waterproof matches. The surface visible in the photograph displays a wipe-off calendar marked with the days of the week. The lower part of the box folds out yet again to provide a writing surface and a couple of well-hidden compartments. Perhaps indiscreet correspondence was projected for young Samuel, who appears to have used other supplies for his letters, including his thank-you note for this elegant gift.

Leather, ivory, and steel writing compendium,
Toulmin and Gale, London, 1881
YALE R. BURGE ANTIQUES

George Catlin, North American Indians, *Edinburgh, 1903;*
William Henry Bartlett, American Scenery, *London, 1840*
BAUMAN RARE BOOKS
Bronze bookends, American, c. 1885
MAN-TIQUES LTD.

BOOKS DO FURNISH A ROOM

In addition to the family Bible, a set of
Shakespeare (possibly cleaned up by
Thomas Bowdler, who removed "those
words and expressions. . .which cannot
with propriety be read aloud in a
family"), and various popular novels, a
middle-class library might contain a
number of books pertaining to the interests of the gentleman of the house.

Heavily illustrated with black-and-
white engravings or etchings, these
volumes are ancestors of today's coffee-
table books. *North American Indians* by
George Catlin is a 1903 edition from
Edinburgh of a book first published
years earlier. George Catlin, an American
artist, traveled extensively through
North America in the 1830s and made
many watercolor paintings of the Indians
he saw. These were later reproduced as
etchings in this book, first published in
1841. The other two volumes are William
Henry Bartlett's *American Scenery*, published in London in 1840. Bartlett was a
landscape artist who traveled all over the
world. This book includes pictures of
various American landmarks such as
Yale College and the Brooklyn Ferry, as
well as scenic landscapes.

Europeans were fascinated by the wild
and rugged aspects of the American continent, and visitors to this country were
usually most impressed by the crisp,
clean air and the spectacular natural features. American attempts at civilization
usually left them unmoved.

The wonders of the New World not-
withstanding, the gentlemen depicted
on the bookends are revered English
authors, Shakespeare and Dickens.

THE WILD WEST

The popular fascination with America's West persisted long after its wild days were done. These carefully detailed statues of American Indians date from 1902 and 1907, when the tribesmen painted by George Catlin (see opposite page) were no longer freely roaming the plains.

The artist is Max Bachmann, a contemporary of Frederic Remington. A native of New York State, Remington built a very successful career as a painter, illustrator, and sculptor by recording (and, it must be admitted, glamorizing) the denizens of the vanishing West. Portrayals of noble Indians and courageous cowboys made Remington a rich man. And his paintings and sculpture pieces are avidly collected to this day.

Bachmann is considerably less famous, but these sculptures, with their giallo antico marble plinths, aim more toward art than craft. Even in their day, they would have been a cut above the usual decorative statuary created for the parlor trade.

The buffalo, however, fits squarely into that market. Ironically enough, he was made in Vienna for export, probably to America, or perhaps for the European market that enjoyed depictions of the American Wild West. The Vienna bronze industry was very sensitive to fashion, or what we would call today "market-driven."

Bronze statues depicting Native Americans on giallo antico marble plinths,
Max Bachmann, American, 1909 and 1902
CLIFFORD BARON
Bronze buffalo statuette, Vienna, late 19th century
HOFFMAN-GAMPETRO ANTIQUES

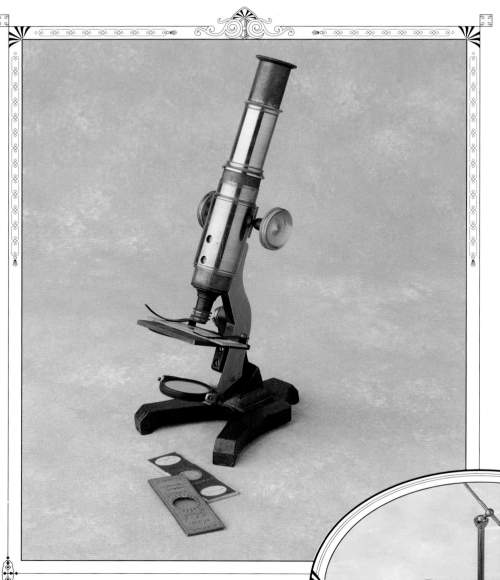

*Brass and cast-iron microscope,
late 19th century; Specimen slides, 1878*
E. BUK
*Silver-mounted specimen glass, French, c. 1890;
Wood-framed magnifying glass, English, c. 1850;
Coddington lens, English, c. 1850*
LYME REGIS, LTD.
Brass-framed magnifying glass, late 19th century
E. BUK

SECOND SIGHT

The well-educated gentleman in pursuit of natural phenomena was a fairly standard phenomenon himself in the nineteenth century. The sciences were in their infancy, and the years of training that make professional scientists today were nonexistent. Discovering a fossil or a previously unseen organism was a possibility for the amateur scientist. (The first dinosaur was unearthed in a gravel pit in the 1820s by Sussex Doctor Gideon Mantell, who was out driving with his wife.)

Owning a microscope was not an everyday thing, but it was probably more common than it is today. A paterfamilias might retire to his slides after dinner the way today's father retreats to The Game or The Paper.

Other forms of optical aid could assist the scholar. The brass-framed "bull's-eye condenser" was used in conjunction with the microscope to bounce an intense ray of light through the slide. The round box is a specimen glass. You pop in your bug and take a magnified look at him. The thick lens with a silver handle is a Coddington lens; it provides very strong magnification and was probably meant for use in the field. The wood-framed glass was used simply for reading. In spite of the development of advanced optical tools like telescopes and microscopes, satisfactory everyday eyeglasses were very much a thing of the future.

GOING STAG

The collector needed a place to store his collection, of course. Scores of vitrines and cabinets from the nineteenth century survive, with their myriad shallow drawers or their felt-lined shelves and cubbyholes. This florid version is distinguished by its hunting motif.

Furniture and crafts made with antlers were indigenous to eastern Germany. Antler chandeliers go back to the early fifteenth century, antler chairs to the late eighteenth century. Queen Victoria had a set of German antler furniture in her Isle of Wight villa, Osborne House. The backs and legs of the chairs were made of sets of antlers and must have been extremely uncomfortable, not to mention hard on ladies' skirts. The Queen's settee, which has an upholstered back, stands on cloven deer hoofs. This style of furniture never became widespread in England or America.

But horn carved well and was sometimes used as a substitute for ivory in items like shoehorns and letter openers, or as ornament for pieces like this cabinet. It is festooned with remarkably symmetrical horntips and horn medallions carved with stags. Even the feet it stands on are made of horn. It is possible that the cabinet itself was a kind of trophy, made from the antlers of animals its owner had killed.

Oak and horn curio cabinet, German, late 19th century
COLLECTION JAMES BEELAND ROGERS, JR.

GOOD SPIRITS

Just as the Victorians ate more than we do, so did they drink more. Although public awareness of the hazards of drink was growing, the temperance movement was aimed at the working class. Men who drank in saloons and reeled home reeking on a Saturday night were the ones who needed to be saved. Men who drank in their clubs or homes and had to be put to bed by the butler were not considered to be at risk.

In fact, a certain amount of alcoholic bonhomie was de rigueur when upper-class men gathered safely away from the restricting influence of women. Thus, men sat and drank port at the dining room table after the ladies had departed. Or they huddled together in the library or smoking room, sipping whiskey or brandy. (Gin, in those days, was a proletarian drink and vodka was virtually unknown.)

Though the term "cocktail" was used in the Victorian era, mixed drinks served over ice didn't become widely popular until this century. Gentlemen poured their spirits straight from handsome cut glass decanters like these, or perhaps added just a splash of soda water. Of course the well-equipped host always had a corkscrew handy for opening up fresh supplies.

Cut glass decanters, English, c. 1860-70
YALE R. BURGE ANTIQUES
Bone with sterling silver corkscrew; Antler with silver plate corkscrew;
Bone with sterling silver corkscrew, all late 19th century
MAN-TIQUES LTD.

A Thing Of Beauty

This splendid jug was a trophy presented at an agricultural show in 1889. The inscription engraved on the lady's long neck reads "The Farmer's Cup Presented by Captain E. 'Pellier' Johnson, Won by Mr. G.H. Stock's 'Shamrock,' April 1889." The lady's diadem serves as a spout and the handle is formed from a twisted hank of her hair.

She is a striking example of the Victorian standard of beauty, and her face actually resembles the face on the contemporaneous (1886) Statue of Liberty. The straight nose with no indentation at the bridge was considered the apogee of the "Grecian" style of beauty. The fullness of her cheeks looks a little heavy to eyes accustomed to high cheekbones and well-defined jaws, but maternal plumpness was fashionable in those days. It was not until the twenties, when women began to break out of the wife-and-mother mold, that slenderness came into style.

Silver plate presentation jug, English, 1889
KENTSHIRE GALLERIES

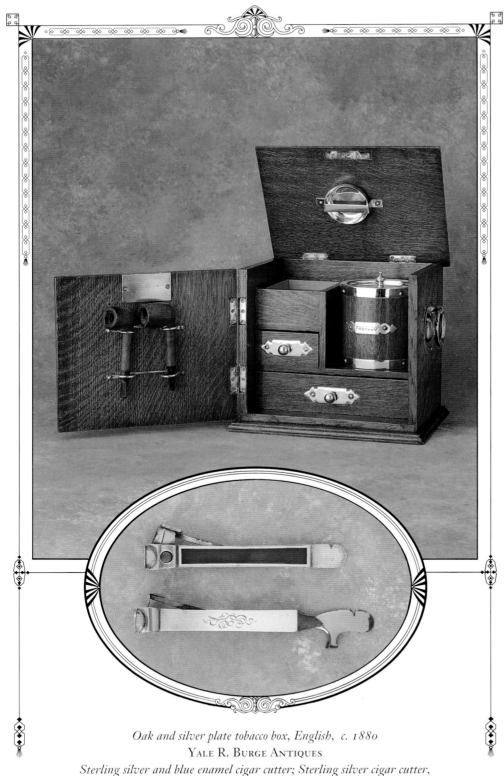

Oak and silver plate tobacco box, English, c. 1880
YALE R. BURGE ANTIQUES
*Sterling silver and blue enamel cigar cutter; Sterling silver cigar cutter,
both late 19th century*
MAN-TIQUES LTD.

TOBACCO ROAD

To conservatives, one of the most shocking harbingers of a new era appeared when, in the early twentieth century, women began to smoke. Throughout the nineteenth century, smoking had been such a masculine activity that when a man smoking a cigar outdoors met a woman he knew, he had to discreetly dispose of the cigar rather than defile her presence with tobacco.

A great deal of paraphernalia grew up around the activity of smoking. Upper-class men would take off their dinner jackets and put on a special "smoking" jacket so that the smell of smoke wouldn't cling to the clothes they wore among ladies. Some of them even wore decorative hats to keep the odorous smoke from their carefully oiled hair.

Even today, many pipe smokers admit that it is the ritual of smoking rather than the intake of tobacco that they really enjoy. This neatly fitted tobacco chest lends credence to that claim. The silver-banded barrel is a humidor, so-called because it keeps the tobacco moist (or "humid"). There are drawers for matches and the tools pipe smokers use for tamping the tobacco and scraping out the ash. There is even, in the lid, a small ashtray.

Cigars require a less elaborate ritual, but the tightly wrapped tips must be cut off to allow the smoke to draw properly. These elegant silver cutters also have broad blades that were used to pry open the wooden boxes that packaged fine cigars.

SMOKE AND FIRE

Matches were still a fairly recent invention (and relatively expensive) in the Victorian era. Technical developments changed their composition throughout the era, and the match industry competed heavily for purchasers. Brand loyalty was strengthened by packing matches in handsome wooden boxes with trademarked designs that featured landmarks such as lighthouses or public events such as sports contests. If a gentleman wanted just a handful of matches to light his cigars while he was away from home, he filled an elegant little match safe from the big box.

Match safes came in many different materials and designs, though the hinged-lid box shape (clearly the ancestor of the Zippo lighter) predominates. These four safes, as well as the ram's horn cigar lighter, exhibit the popular Victorian snake or dragon motif. In all of the match safes the sinuous, fluid lines of the serpent have been cleverly integrated into the basic rectangle of the matchbox. The top left and bottom right safes, exquisitely detailed, compress two dragons (on the left) or a single long snake (on the right) into the requisite box shape. The top right safe ties a serpent with a lion's head neatly around the box, while the bottom left snake pierces the box, as if you might find his coils inside.

The cigar lighter represents a mythical beast with an eagle's head, bird's legs, and the body of a serpent. Using an ingenious system of wicks and fuel, this creature could be set to "breathe fire" and thereby provide low flames for an entire evening's worth of cigars. The thoughtful host would thus spare his guests from using their own matches.

Sterling silver match safes, late 19th century
ILENE CHAZANOF
Silver plate and horn cigar lighter, late 19th century
LINDA HORN ANTIQUES

Silver plate and brass-cased clock and barometer set
with white onyx bases, English, c. 1870
KENTSHIRE GALLERIES

MARKING TIME

Measuring was an important theme in the latter half of the nineteenth century, and measuring time precisely was a particularly great concern in America because of the country's great size. For most of the century, towns and cities across the country set their public clocks by the sun. Since the sun appears to move from east to west, Sacramento (for example) was nearly four minutes behind San Francisco. When the country was joined by railroads, however, schedules became unbearably complicated. In 1883, an attempt was made to organize the country into unified time zones with Standard Railway Time. In spite of energetic protesters who felt that standard time was a heartless and dehumanizing notion, it took hold. In the new industrial world, time was money.

If standard time was a harbinger of the future, dependence on the weather was a relic of the past. Farmers and small producers were gravely affected by the state of the heavens, but to the middle-class man who would have placed this handsome clock and barometer set on his desk, predictions of "rain" or "fine" would dictate only whether or not he took an umbrella with him to the office. In a startling reversal of age-old circumstances, by the late nineteenth century, weather was more likely to affect the average man's leisure than his working hours.

POSTAGE DUE

We think of the Victorian era as a great age for writing letters, and two very specific inventions made it that way. One was the envelope, the other one was the postage stamp.

Britain was the pioneer nation, introducing the Penny Post (and the stamp) in 1840. Until then, the cost to mail a letter was quite high (for instance, eleven pence from London to Liverpool) and varied with both distance and weight. Moreover, the *receiver* often paid to get letters. To save money, correspondents frequently "crossed" their letters, writing horizontally on the paper, then turning and writing vertically.

The Penny Post did away with this, charging a penny for any letter up to half an ounce in weight. It took the U.S. seven years to get on the stamp bandwagon, but in 1847, five-cent Ben Franklin stamps and ten-cent George Washingtons appeared. The cost of postage dropped through the century.

The manufacture of envelopes began in the late 1830s, but they weren't widely used while correspondents had to pay extra postage for the additional weight of the envelope. The more usual procedure was to seal a sheet of paper with wax. The slender upright part of the inkstand here was probably used to hold the writer's seal, though sealing wax was really just a decorative flourish on correspondence by the time the inkstand was made.

Sterling silver and glass inkstand, c. 1860
COLLECTION KATHRYN LICHTER
Sterling silver postal scale, Pelouze, Chicago, 1898
MAN-TIQUES LTD.

To Have And To Hold

They were great accumulators, the Victorians, and they had a greater tolerance for cluttered surfaces than we do. But at some point things have to be put away. For instance, all those letters. The manila folder and the filing cabinet didn't make an appearance until the end of the century, and then only in offices. Handsome rolltop desks with compartments and pigeonholes were similarly confined to the business world, and the separation between work and home was extremely distinct in those days.

The U.S. Government bundled up its correspondence with red cloth tape and bound it into chronological volumes, but this system was not an option for the average householder. Instead, he simply stored his letters in boxes.

These are particularly handsome examples. The box in the inset is made of porcupine quills with ebony and ivory decorations. It was probably crafted in India for export, and since many boxes in this style survive, we can assume that they were quite popular.

The box in the main photograph is quite grand. Made of leather, it is decorated with engraved bronze acanthus-shaped appliques. The hinged lid is adorned with an oval agate. This box also locks, so it was clearly used for precious contents.

Leather, bronze, and agate box, late 19th century
PRIVATE COLLECTION
Porcupine quill, ebony, and ivory box, probably Indian, late 19th century
ANTIQUE CACHE

WORLD VIEW

If your mantel is graced by a pair of
Bohemian glass vases, you just might
want to know where Bohemia is. Likewise,
if you have just bought a set of stereographs of the great cathedrals of France,
you might want to know the exact where-
abouts of Reims. A globe was a necessity
for a family that wanted to cultivate a
worldly view.

For us, living in the global village,
linked by satellite to the far sides of the
earth, this may seem humdrum. But a
hundred years ago, awareness of foreign
places was new and rather thrilling. The
mapping of Africa and South America
was not yet complete. Steamships that
crossed oceans in days instead of weeks
were still a novelty. When newspaperman
(later explorer) Henry Stanley found the
lost explorer Dr. David Livingstone in a
remote African village in 1871, it took
months for the news to reach New York.
When it did, it was, in the new parlance,
a scoop, because the explorer was a great
public figure. Exotic places had immense
glamour, possibly comparable to the
glamour generated by space exploration
in this century.

This globe has considerable glamour
of its own. Manufactured by Rand-
McNally, the longtime American map-
makers, it stands on a handsome tripod.
The cast-iron base and feet are formed
in an eighteenth-century revival style,
but the balls of the ball and claw feet
are, appropriately enough, globes.

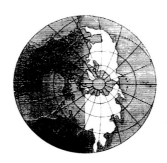

Terrestrial globe, Rand-McNally, American, c. 1900
ACCENTS UNLIMITED, LTD.

Ballet dancer animated shadowbox, German, c. 1885
HILLMAN-GEMINI ANTIQUES

DANCING GIRLS

This deep, mirrored box makes an ideal stage for the dancers inside it, who actually twirl when the box is wound. Large numbers of automated toys like this were manufactured in the U.S. and Europe, but this one is probably too sophisticated to have been meant for the nursery.

What is striking about the dancers is their costume. Their skirts, though held stiffly away from the hips by a petticoat or hoop, are extremely short. Pantalettes give them a measure of modesty, but they are nevertheless exposing far more of their ankles than is proper. This is, after all, the era that insisted on referring to "limbs" rather than legs. It seems likely that this tableau might have been placed in the library to give gentlemen a little thrill as they smoked.

A hundred years ago, ballet was not the highbrow entertainment that it is today. Although classics of the repertoire such as *Giselle* were performed in America earlier in the century, by the 1880s ballet had degenerated into a mere diversion. Dances might be performed as preludes to theatrical pieces, and the staging of most operas included dancing in the third act. But while opera companies were heavily patronized by the social elite, the audience for dance was a bit *louche*. What they appreciated was less the refinement and skill of the performance than a mild level of titillation.

GREAT SCOTT

Sir Walter Scott was a Scottish poet and novelist whose work, produced in the first third of the nineteenth century, remained hugely popular for several generations. He wrote narrative poetry and romantic historical novels, most of them set in long-ago Scotland. He was immensely prolific: the *Waverley* series, the first of which was about Bonnie Prince Charlie, ran to thirty-two titles. Other famous Scott works include *Ivanhoe, Guy Mannering, Rob Roy,* and *The Bride of Lammermoor* (later the basis for a Donizetti opera, *Lucia di Lammermoor*).

Scott's work is little read today; the plots seem far-fetched and the style is stilted. But the nineteenth-century longing for the picturesque and the romantic was satisfied by Scott's wild Highland settings, noble heroes, and beleaguered heroines.

The veneration of Scott lasted through the Victorian era, as these objects attest. The miniature portrait bust, about four inches tall, is made of Parian porcelain, a fine semimatte porcelain that was supposed to mimic marble. Parian was most often used for statuettes and other decorative items. It was well suited for reproducing details; here Scott seems to be wearing a plaid, the broad length of tartan worn draped around the shoulders in rustic Scotland.

The silk tartan-bound books are copies of Scott's narrative poem *Marmion* and an adapted version of his *Mary, Queen of Scots.* The bust dates from around 1880, the books from around 1890, nearly sixty years after Scott's death in 1832.

Tartan-covered books, English, c. 1890;
Parian ware bust, English, c. 1880
LYME REGIS, LTD.

THE *Dining Room*

*The hostess who gives good dinners is
pretty sure to succeed in social life,
and will be almost certain to
marry her daughters well.*

MRS. HUMPHRY, *Manners for Women*, 1897

Dining room, Residence of Mrs. Mayer, 1896
Museum of the City of New York
The Byron Collection
Background wallpaper design: Schumacher

*T*he mere possession of a separate room consecrated to dining was a badge, in the Victorian era, of membership in the middle class. Less prosperous families might eat in their kitchens, or perhaps in a combination parlor and dining room. It was only the well-to-do who could devote both the space and the capital to furnish a dining room.

Dining—it was never just eating—was taken very seriously by the Victorians, and their dining rooms were furnished accordingly. Since the dining room would be used mostly at night, it was important that the wall colors be rich, so that they would show up well by candlelight. Even for luncheons, curtains were drawn. Dramatic views and excessive "glare" from outdoors were thought to distract from the serious business at hand. Furniture was rather massive in style, usually in mahogany or another dark wood. A substantial table was necessary, of course, as were multiple chairs. Eight was a standard number, since anyone who had a dining room would inevitably use it for entertaining. There was also a sideboard, used primarily for displaying massive pieces of silver such as trays or candelabras.

Although all of the planning and ordering of meals was the housewife's responsibility, the dining room had a distinctly masculine tone. Formal entertaining is, by its very nature, ostentatious, with its display of silver and china and many-coursed meals of rich foods. It implies wealth. And wealth, in those days, was strictly a man's concern. While his wife must be educated enough to spend money in the right way, it was his labor that produced the money in the first place.

Of course, entertaining required a great deal of effort from the lady of the house as well. Giving a dinner party not only presented an opportunity to show off wealth; it was also a ritual of class solidarity. In the highest circles, where social competition was fierce, deviation from the norm was risky. If crimson American Beauty roses were in fashion, heaven help the lady who decked her table with last year's choice, the yellow Jacqueminot rose. If New York fashion dictated that Roman punch between courses be flavored with kirsch, the lady whose punch tasted of rum showed herself to be woefully ignorant.

Participation in a formal dinner was taxing for guests, too, of course. There was a great deal of anxiety about manners in the Victorian era, as there is in any time of increased social mobility. New aspirants to the middle class suspected their savoir faire might be a bit lacking, so they made an eager audience for scores of etiquette manuals. Although these volumes devote adequate coverage to the intricacies of introductions and paying calls and behavior on the dance floor, they invariably linger on table manners. Then as now, there was a great deal of confusion about what to do with all those forks.

Negotiating dinner was made more difficult in the late nineteenth century by the new convention known as "French service." Until the 1830s or '40s, the principal dishes of a course were all put on the table at once. Diners helped each other to dishes that were out of reach, which gave a note of communal informality to the proceedings. But at the Russian court, dishes were served one at a time, and the habit soon spread to Paris, and thence to the United States.

The most common complaint about French service—that guests did not know what was coming, or might not recognize it when it appeared—was solved by the introduction of menu cards. These were usually handwritten by the hostess (it was considered

Very few diners work straight through a menu without omitting some dishes. The idea of giving so many is that there may be some to suit all tastes.

Mrs. Humphry, *Manners for Men*, 1897

To be acquainted with every detail of the etiquette pertaining to the dinner party is of the highest importance to every lady. A young woman who elects to take claret with her fish, or eat peas with her knife, justly risks being banished from good society.

Collier's Cyclopedia of Commercial and Social Information, 1883

vulgar to have a secretary write them) and placed between each pair of diners. It was essential to read them quickly before dinner began, because sometimes diners were offered a choice, as between cream or clear soup.

The Victorian menus that have survived are a bit misleading; diners did not partake of all the courses mentioned. Sometimes, as in the soup course, they could select one of two or more options. Nevertheless, their meals were much heavier than ours. A dinner served at Marlborough House, the Prince of Wales' residence, in December of 1883, began with oysters, then a choice of soups (turtle or consomme with ravioli). Lobster puffs made a brief interlude, followed by the fish course (turbot with hollandaise sauce). Then came a choice of *entrées*, also known as "dressed dishes." These were usually rather elaborate meat dishes. In the case of the Prince's dinner, the choice was creamed partridges or mutton cutlets. The next course—and the end was nowhere in sight—offered a choice of tarragon chicken or roast venison. Then came roast pheasant served with artichokes, followed by a choice of bavarian cream or an orange jelly. Ice cream finished the meal.

In the grandest houses, these elaborate dinners were served entirely by servants. A butler and several gloved, liveried footmen proffered dishes and, at a nod from the diner, placed the appropriate serving on the plate. In the middle-class home, however, diners had to do more work, and things could be more complicated. A maid might offer a dish around the table, but diners had to serve themselves. So how many potatoes should one take? Were the croquettes going to skid off that extremely slippery plate? Would there be enough soup to go around?

Then, at every level of society, there were those awkward foods that required specific tools or tricky techniques. What did the genteel diner do with cherry pits? What was the best way to eat quail? Exactly how did one manage a marrow spoon? Many of the etiquette books of the era discuss these issues in a sympathetic way. "The young diner-out," proclaims one volume, "often finds dessert the most trying course of all. It is so difficult to eat fruit gracefully, she thinks, and I am not sure she is not right."

At the same time, conversation must be kept going, also along strictly defined lines. Only the most innocuous subjects were acceptable, and general chatter across the table was unheard of. At the beginning of the meal, the hostess began conversing with the gentleman on her right, and the other ladies opened discussion with the gentlemen on their right. They talked through the first course, and then, as the next was served, the hostess began talking to the man at her left. This was called "turning the table," for the

other ladies followed suit, each turning to talk to the man on her other side.

At the end of the meal, the hostess put her napkin on the table, gathered up her gloves, looked at the other ladies, and stood up. All the gentlemen stood as well, pulling back chairs as the ladies filed from the table. The tablecloth was removed, leaving the gleaming mahogany bare, and decanters of port and brandy were circulated (always clockwise; counterclockwise was bad luck).

While the ladies clustered together in the ornate, feminine parlor, the men lingered in the sober confines of the dining room, discussing the really important things in life—like horses and the stock market.

FINE DINING

This is the kind of place setting that gives modern diners great anxiety. All those forks! All those glasses! What's it all for? In 1860, everybody just knew. (Everybody in the middle class, that is.)

The tiny fork on the right is a tarpon fork, used for the fish that was considered a great delicacy and was sometimes served as a first course. The other two forks and knives were used as the diner worked his way through the menu. English writer E.F. Benson writes of dinners his parents gave in the 1870s, remembering that after fish and soup came entrées (dishes made of meat), then a joint or roast, then birds, either duck or game, followed by "substantial puddings," then cheese, then dessert (which was usually fruit). Wines, of course, were served to complement the food. Sherry usually went with soup, then a white wine, then a red, with different glasses for each. Since servants did the pouring, managing glassware was simple.

The dessert setting in the smaller photograph includes a scalloped ice-cream spoon as well as a fork and teaspoon. The shallow glass is for champagne, the small glass for cordials. The cutlery is all medallion silver (see opposite page) and the china, dating from the 1830s, is ironstone, hand-painted in the traditional "Imari" colors of dark and light blues with terra cotta.

Ironstone covered vegetable dish, dinner plate, and dessert plate, English, c. 1830; Stemware, English, c. 1880; Glass condiment dish, English, c. 1840; Glass pitcher, English, c. 1860
BARDITH LTD.
Medallion silver cutlery, John Wendt, New York, after 1862; Medallion silver mustard pot, salt cellar, and pepper shaker, American, late 19th century; Mother-of-pearl handled knife, late 19th century
PRIVATE COLLECTION

SERVE YOURSELF

Some of the most bewildering remnants of Victorian culture are the serving pieces that accompanied sets of silver flatware. All of the pieces pictured here are made in a very well-documented pattern of medallion silver, a style of American silver flatware first produced in 1862. It was highly popular in the 1860s, a period when ancient Greek and Roman styles were fashionable. Various manufacturers produced medallion silver throughout the century, and though the revived and recast versions from the 1880s have stylistic differences from the originals of the 1860s, they all bear classical portraits in medallions on the handles.

These pieces were produced by John Wendt and were the first pattern of medallion silver to receive a U.S. patent. Wendt's design is quite simple, with cleanly stamped right-facing portraits in oval frames, each decorated with a circular finial. Manufacturers' marks identify the retailer, and the identity of some of the classical deities in the medallions can even be guessed at. But the functions of these pieces is what remains unclear to all but the most erudite connoisseurs.

The Victorian appetite for specialization resulted in minute variations of the spoon shape for serving different foods. The server at the left of the top row is a cheese scoop, and the pierced spoon next to it is a sugar shaker. The largest piece, at the far left of the bottom row, was probably for serving molded jellies or sandwiches, while the fluted spoons may be a sugar shell for serving from a sugar bowl, and an ice-cream serving spoon. But these identifications are conjectural, and it would take a confident Victorian hostess to set the record straight.

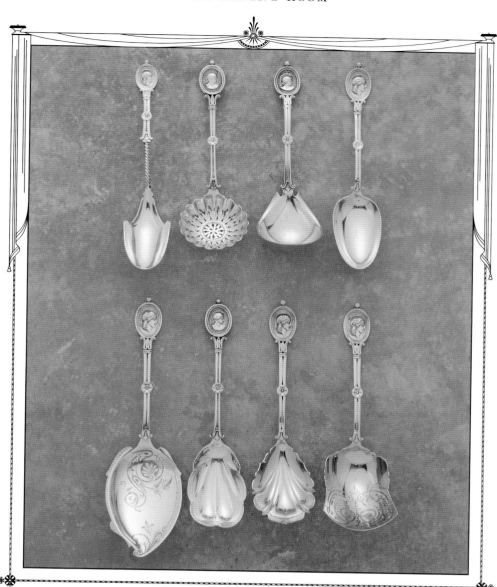

Sterling silver medallion pattern serving pieces,
John Wendt, American, after 1862
PRIVATE COLLECTION

Silver plate and green glass butter dish, American, c. 1860
KENTSHIRE GALLERIES

BOVINE BEAUTY

Although this silver plate and glass butter dish falls into many of the same categories as the cranberry glass on the opposite page (silver and glass, tableware, novelty serving piece), in design terms it is a very different affair. While the silver top of the sugar caster is simple, and the lid, stand, and spoon of the jam dish carry out a whimsical theme, the elaborate pierced work on this butter dish exhibits mixed motifs. The handles, with their sinuous loops and curlicues, emulate wrought metal. The feet, meanwhile, imitate the paw feet sometimes found on eighteenth-century furniture. Whose paws?

The three-dimensional pattern running around the side of the dish is formed of curlicues and tassels. The top band is larger than the bottom band, though the proportional difference is not immediately obvious. The pierced silver on the top is flat, abstract, vaguely Gothic. And surmounting it all—a cow, perhaps to signal what the dish contains. Maybe the glass is green to remind users of what the cow ate?

This dizzying confection of ornament is the kind of thing that design reformers railed against, but in all their earnestness they made no allowance for charm. The source of delight? Maybe it's the cow; maybe it's the paws after all. Or maybe it's the grassy green of the glass, which would make the butter look very appealing indeed.

PRETTY IN PINK

These three pieces of cranberry glass exhibit an engaging modesty characteristic of the early to mid-Victorian period. This may be because they fall chronologically between two waves of manufacturing innovation. When the technique of pouring or pressing molten glass into molds appeared in the 1830s, the first molded glass imitated the allover geometric patterns of expensive handmade cut glass. By mid-century, the novelty value of pressed glass had faded, and the surfaces calmed down. The sugar caster is simply faceted, and the cheese dish has a restrained, incised band of Greek-key decoration on both cover and plate.

Cranberry-colored glass was popular during this period. This rosy shade of pink was much loved, appearing on Staffordshire lusterware (see the plaques on page 40), on chintzes and wallpapers and carpets. The frosted cranberry glass looks forward to the technical jamboree in glassmaking later in the century, when shading, cutting, enameling, crimping and casing produced fantastic and elaborate results.

The combination of glass and silver, represented in both the sugar caster and the jam dish, was popular throughout the period, but the simplicity of these pieces is forward-looking and, to our eyes, quite modern. The leaf-shaped stand and spoon of the jam dish and the "twigs" on the railing of the stand are completely smooth, with no modeling. Their glossy skin seems to hint at the direction that Christopher Dresser (see pages 84 and 85) would soon take in his silver and glass designs.

Frosted cranberry glass cheese dish, English, c. 1870
KENTSHIRE GALLERIES
Cranberry glass and silver plate sugar caster, English, c. 1870;
Cranberry glass and silver plate jam dish, English, c. 1860
KENTSHIRE GALLERIES

Earthenware compote, English, c. 1870
PRIVATE COLLECTION

CLASSICAL IMAGERY

One strong link between the late eighteenth century and the period that followed was a reverence for the civilizations of ancient Greece and Rome. This ceramic compote, with its band of geometric decoration and the central motif of three vases, makes allusions to the theme of archaeology.

This is rather modest tableware. The design was probably transfer-printed and then hand-colored, a less expensive means of decorating than hand-painting. The pattern is fairly common in antique stores, indicating that it must have been quite popular. So thousands of middle-class families scooped their croquettes off tableware decorated with old vases. Why? Why was archaeology appealing?

One answer is that the ongoing excavation of classical sites like Pompeii and Herculaneum held out great excitement. Investigation of ancient domestic life was thrilling to people who placed much emphasis on their own domestic habits.

Another factor is that this was an era of revivals. Throughout the nineteenth century, numerous books on the decorative arts of other cultures appeared, and many of them were aimed at the decorating trade. Owen Jones' *The Grammar of Ornament* (1856) provided information on nineteen styles, including "Hindoo," "The Ornament of Savage Tribes," and "Celtic." This "Etruscan" compote might have been tame in comparison, but it was considerably more exciting than an old bunch of flowers.

A ROUND DOZEN

This set of gilded silver spoons harks back to a style that was first made in the fifteenth century, the apostle spoon. In their earliest form, apostle spoons were made singly. The bowl of the spoon was round, and the little figure at the end of the handle was iconographically identifiable as one of the twelve original followers of Jesus. These spoons were often given as christening gifts.

Very few complete sets of twelve spoons have survived from the Renaissance, and one known as the "Stirling Set" was exhibited in London in 1862, possibly sparking interest in the form. Certainly, twelve was a convenient number for spoons, the Renaissance was picturesque, and a Victorian revival of apostle spoons was therefore hardly surprising.

This set of spoons, dated 1868, artfully mixes both old and new. The use of gilding was faithful to the antique prototypes, as was the twisted form of the handle. The oval bowls of the spoons, however, are much more modern—characteristic of a typical Victorian teaspoon. Some sets of early apostle spoons were made with a thirteenth spoon featuring a figure of Jesus; this was known as the "master spoon." The round-bowled sugar spoon at the center of this case, a sugar spoon, may be a Victorian adaptation. The sugar tongs, clearly, are a handsome but anachronistic concession to the realities of lump sugar.

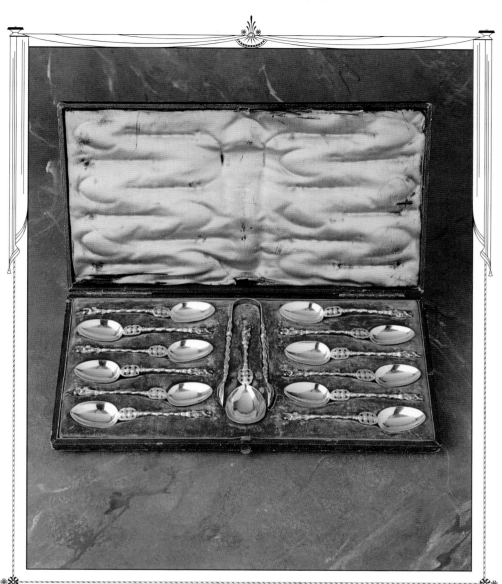

Gilt over sterling silver apostle spoons, sugar spoon, and tongs, London, 1868
D.K. BRESSLER & COMPANY

Majolica shell plates, English, late 19th century
COLLECTION JUDY SINGER
Sterling silver medallion-patterned cutlery,
George W. Shiebler, American, c. 1880
PRIVATE COLLECTION
Sterling silver napkin rings,
George W. Shiebler, American, c. 1880
ILENE CHAZANOF
Majolica fish pitchers, English, late 19th century
COLLECTION JUDY SINGER

FISH STORY

Majolica was one of the most popular kinds of pottery in the Victorian era. It was produced first in England around the middle of the century; potters were emulating a sixteenth-century Italian ware known as *maiolica*. The Victorian form is molded earthenware, almost always in naturalistic shapes. Much of it, like the pieces shown here and opposite, is tableware.

The molds were usually quite detailed (witness the scales on the fish pitchers in the small photograph, or the grasses on the spoon warmer opposite). Glazes, usually in a limited palette of greens, browns, pinks, and blues, might or might not be realistic. The deep green and brown on the shell plates here is more characteristic of English majolica than of American wares, whose glazes were usually more transparent.

The shell plates are shown here as part of a table setting for, naturally, a fish course. These broad-bladed knives and asymmetrical forks were made just for eating fish: one tine is wider, to form a small blade on its own. This is typical of the urge toward specialization so characteristic of the era.

Though an etiquette book published in 1837 states, "Fish does not require a knife, but should be divided by the aid of a piece of bread," it wasn't long before special cutlery for fish was a badge of prosperity. In a classic display of snobbery, English aristocratic families considered fish knives and forks nouveau riche, and therefore quite beneath their dignity.

FULL OF SPOONS

This extremely unusual object is a spoon warmer. The egg is filled with hot water, and spoons are placed inside to be warmed up. It probably dates from around 1860, when this particular refinement of etiquette was in vogue. Most spoon warmers were produced in silver plate, and this majolica version, with its bulrushes theme, is very rare.

Spoon warmers, by and large, are not common, so the practice of warming spoons must not have lasted long. (Perhaps warmed spoons were used for soup?) In general, upper- and upper-middle-class manners at this time were very elaborate. Etiquette, particularly table manners, has always been used as a way to stress solidarity and to distinguish outsiders from a group.

In the mid-nineteenth century, an era of great social mobility, the upper class developed a number of rituals that would distinguish those in the know. The great profusion of utensils in the average Victorian table setting, which would confound most modern diners, served to brand nouveau riche aspirants to society as uncouth. Anecdotes about rubes drinking the contents of finger bowls abound. Perhaps the arcane spoon warmer was another one of these hurdles for the upwardly mobile.

Majolica spoon warmer,
English, c. 1860
HOFFMAN-GAMPETRO ANTIQUES

Porcelain foo dogs, Chinese, c. 1860
KENTSHIRE GALLERIES
Imari-style pitchers, Mason's Patent Ironstone,
English, c. 1860
KENTSHIRE GALLERIES

ORIENTAL STYLE

Porcelain from the Far East had always been highly valued in Europe, and in the early nineteenth century, many a Western manufacturer began attempting to reproduce both the fine translucence of Oriental porcelain and the distinctive styles of its glazes. The plates on page 72, for example, are very similar to these pitchers in color scheme. But in the 1830s when those plates were made, "Japanese" style was a rather far-fetched version of the original, since Japan had been closed to the West for two hundred years.

These ironstone pitchers, manufactured around 1860, show more legitimate Oriental influence. The pattern is more asymmetrical, the shapes of the flowers closer to traditional stylized Japanese form. This may be a result of renewed Western trade with Japan, negotiated in 1854 by the American Commodore Matthew Perry. Certainly, in the 1860s, after the British Minister to Japan exhibited his collection of Japanese artifacts in London, the design community began to focus very seriously on Oriental objects, and Japanese influence was widespread for the next twenty years.

While the pitchers were manufactured in England in the Japanese style, the foo dogs were made in China for export. Foo dogs, also sometimes known as "lion dogs," were reputed to be extremely courageous and were used as temple guardians. They are usually depicted in this fierce, fangs-exposed pose, though some examples, probably intended to depict females, have a foo puppy climbing onto the raised front foot. Owing to the Victorian passion for animals and the equally strong Victorian passion for the exotic, foo dog statues were highly prized.

SEASON TO TASTE

The caster set, also known as a cruet set, was a decorative response to the Victorian palate's preference for strong seasoning. Even the simplest version, like the charming wagonload of barrels in the inset photograph, included a salt shaker, a pepper shaker, and a mustard pot (though not, confusingly enough, a caster or a cruet). More elaborate sets, like the one in the large picture, provided for more complex taste sensations.

This example sports two silver-topped bottles, two bottles with glass stoppers, two squat jars, and a bell for summoning the maid. The bottles would probably have contained oil, vinegar, and perhaps two varieties of the seasoning known as "ketchup," a home-bottled preserve usually based on tomatoes, mushrooms, or walnuts. The jars might have contained homemade chutney (often pickled from garden leftovers) and prepared mustard.

This set apparently graced the table at a Catholic rectory in Pennsylvania, for an inscription engraved around the center post reads, "Presented by the Rev. Al Filan to St. Peter's Catholic Church, Elizabethtown, Lancaster Co." A patent date of 1859 is stamped on the center post, establishing the earliest possible date of manufacture.

The "caster" in the name actually refers to a kind of sugar. A hundred years ago, sugar was usually sold in large conical loaves that weighed between five and thirty-five pounds. Lumps were hacked off and broken up as needed. Caster sugar was pounded so fine that it would pour through a shaker, also known as a caster. (Today's powdered sugar is our closest equivalent.) Sugar casters were often made of silver and looked like overgrown salt shakers. They were placed on the table so that diners could sweeten fruit or desserts to their taste.

Silver plate and glass caster set, American, after 1859
MAN-TIQUES LTD.
Oak and silver plate caster set, English, c. 1870
KENTSHIRE GALLERIES

Bone-handled carving set with steel blades and sterling silver collars,
English, c. 1860
KENTSHIRE GALLERIES

A Man's Job

Much of the design of the Victorian era has what we think of as a very feminine look. The ornamentation, the colors, the elaborate shapes, and materials seem to be geared more for women than for men. The house, after all, was the woman's province. Its furnishings were supposed to reflect the woman's character.

But some tasks were still emphatically the man's, and carving was one of them. The skillful dissection of roasted birds or joints (what we call roasts) was not as challenging as it had been in the seventeenth century, when a well-bred host might be called on to carve up anything from a carp to a hare. Still, a Victorian gentleman knew never to offer a woman a leg of fowl (it was considered indelicate; men and women weren't supposed to discuss what birds walked on lest somehow they betray knowledge of what women walked on), and to offer her "white meat" rather than "breast."

Mrs. Beeton, in her *Book of Household Management*, presents an idealized Dickensian view of the "respected, portly paterfamilias" carving "his own fat turkey, and carving it well." Times may have changed (portly is no longer a complimentary adjective), but come Thanksgiving, it's usually a man who picks up the carving knife.

ROAST FOWL.

GOOSE.

NECK OF VEAL.

CALF HEAD.

THE WELL-DRESSED TABLE

One Victorian fashion that has yet to be revived is the extraordinarily elaborate decoration of tables. Grand dinners of the 1880s and '90s featured tables set with dozens of flowers in elaborate tiered vases. Candelabras, multiple glasses at each place, complex settings of flatware, napkin rings, cruet sets, bonbon dishes, and place-card holders covered the table in gorgeous profusion. "It is in matters like these," said an etiquette book from 1897, "that the taste of the hostess is clearly shown."

Epergnes were a composite form of table furnishing. They usually combined silver and glass, and could be extremely elaborate. Often they would encompass vases, candle holders, and bonbon or fruit dishes. Tall flower arrangements with trailing fronds of maidenhair fern or smilax were very fashionable. This epergne, with its striated glass vases in the form of flowers and its copper leaf-shaped base, is relatively modest and probably dates from quite late in the century.

The practice of using place cards lingers in formal modern circles, and "seating" a table is still one of the hostess' great headaches. A hundred years ago, table placement was supposed to reflect social standing, so that the highest-ranking male guest sat next to the hostess. (This could cause great tension in America, where social standing was still a matter of opinion.)

These beautifully detailed majolica place-card holders were probably a modish novelty. Water lilies had quite a vogue in the late nineteenth century, and these holders were the kind of pretty, clever innovation that gave a hostess a reputation for being "original."

Glass and copper epergne, late 19th century
COLLECTION BUNNY KOPPELMAN
Majolica place-card holders, late 19th century
LINDA HORN ANTIQUES

MODERN MAN

These sleek articles may look out of place in a book of Victorian design, but they are certifiably of the era—chronologically, at least. They were designed by the visionary Scottish botanist and designer Dr. Christopher Dresser. Having studied both at London's School of Design and at the Royal Botanic Gardens, he was always aware of the geometric shapes behind nature, and his training in botany remained an important influence in his work. His contemporary, Cezanne, said that "Nature must be treated through the cylinder, the sphere, the cone," and Dresser's designs (especially in glass and silver) adhere to this philosophy. His simplicity seems routine to post-modern eyes, but it was startling in the 1880s and '90s when bourgeois taste most admired the ornately elaborate.

Perhaps the most forward-looking element in Dresser's philosophy was his wholehearted adoption of industrial manufacturing. While reformers like William Morris and Charles Eastlake wanted to turn their backs on the artificial perfection that machines produced (always preferring the evidence of the craftsman's hand), Dresser looked forward. Some of his pieces, like this sugar carter, are so sleek they might have been designed in a wind tunnel.

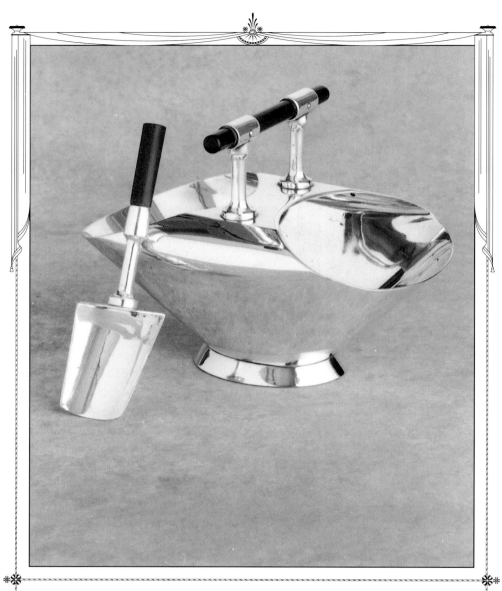

Silver plate and ebony sugar carter,
probably Hukin & Heath,
English, c. 1890
SPLIT PERSONALITY

EMPIRE OF THE SUN

Another very strong influence on Christopher Dresser was his exposure to the crafts of Japan. Although Japanese aesthetics were immensely fashionable in the late nineteenth century, Dresser was the first European designer who actually spent time in the country. He was impressed with the level of craftsmanship, and made a number of innovations that echoed what he found there.

The coffeepot and decanter shown here are typical of Dresser's glass and silver plate tableware. He designed a range of vessels for Hukin & Heath that were manufactured in the 1890s. Many of his decanters (or claret jugs) share this basic design, with a silver spout and lid, and a silver band around the body of the glass, joined by a simple ebony rod. This was a very Japanese element, as were the exposed rivets visible on the collars of the handle.

Another characteristic of Dresser's work is that form, as modernist architect Louis Sullivan said, follows function. Handles and spouts, however geometrically severe, are placed so that the vessels pour easily, a detail some recent designers have often overlooked.

Silver plate and ebony coffeepot;
Glass, silver plate, and ebony decanter,
Hukin & Heath, English, c. 1890
SPLIT PERSONALITY

Papier-mâché tea caddy, English, c. 1840
KENTSHIRE GALLERIES

*Under certain circumstances there
are few hours in life more agreeable
than the hour dedicated to the
ceremony known as afternoon tea.*

HENRY JAMES, *Portrait of a Lady*, 1882

TEA TIME

Papier-mâché was a material much beloved by the craftsmen and consumers of the early to mid-nineteenth century. Sheets of thick paper soaked in glue were laid into molds and baked dry at a very low temperature. Then more sheets were added and dried until the article was thick enough to stand alone and hold its shape. Finally it was coated with shellac and painted, or sometimes inlaid with mother-of-pearl. Although black is the most common background color, other deep hues such as green sometimes appear. The decorative painting is usually multi-colored and features lots of gilding.

Papier-mâché was used for a surprising array of objects (including a piano shown at London's 1851 Great Exhibition that apparently sounded dreadful), but the most successful were small graceful side chairs and decorative accessories: trays (like the one on page 111) and the various boxes the Victorians were so fond of.

This tea caddy is a classic example of papier-mâché craft, with its smooth shape, ornamental feet, and meticulous parrot and flower decoration. It is fitted with two lidded compartments for two varieties of leaves, perhaps China (which produced a mild, pale brew) and India (which made darker, stronger tea). Like all tea caddies, it can be locked to prevent servants from pilfering.

Tea For Two

The ritual of drinking tea and eating a small meal late in the afternoon was an English custom imported to America. It was most popular, however, with the middle and upper classes.

Tea was an ideal time for visiting, and the complex ritual of serving and taking tea was one of those elaborate solidarity procedures. The hazards of slippery cup in slippery saucer, boiling water, one lump or two, removal of gloves, China or India, milk in first—negotiating this mine field correctly gave all of the participants a secure feeling that they belonged in their class. The paraphernalia was as specialized as the ceremonial behavior of using it. The silver tea strainer in the inset photograph would be placed over the cup to catch any stray tea leaves. The cup, with its roses and gilded wreaths, is a classic example of unreconstructed mid-century Victorian taste.

This teapot, on the other hand, embodies the English adoration of Japan that reached a climax in the 1880s. The pot itself, with the exception of the chamfered sides, is fairly conventionally shaped, and most of the gilded ornament is quite Western. But the kimono-clad figure and the saucer, with its curved octagonal shape and sunburst motif, do show incontrovertible Japanese influence.

The English passion for things Japanese reached such a pitch that in 1885 Gilbert and Sullivan lampooned it in one of their most successful operettas, *The Mikado*. The men's opening chorus begins, "If you want to know who we are, We are gentlemen of Japan, On many a vase and jar, on many a screen and fan, We figure in lively paint; Our attitude's queer and quaint." As usual, Gilbert has it exactly right: the "queer and quaint" was an immense part of the appeal.

Ceramic teapot, English, c. 1880
PRIVATE COLLECTION
Hand-painted porcelain cup and saucer, c. 1860;
Sterling silver and ivory tea strainer, late 19th century
PRIVATE COLLECTION

SILVER JUBILEE

This delightful silver wheelbarrow may have had a glass liner that would enable it to be used for flowers, but it might also have held bonbons or nuts. Smaller versions that served as saltcellars were also manufactured; sometimes they included a little Cupid to push the wheelbarrow. An etiquette book from 1897 points out that "delicately tooled silver dishes in pierced work for bonbons are seen on every well-laid table when a dinner party is in question."

This was the kind of article that design reformers despised, however. Its form had nothing to do with its purpose. A gardening implement, no matter how cunningly produced, did not belong on a dining room table. The pierced ornamentation, moreover, belonged to the variety frequently scorned as utterly "meaningless."

The serving fork and spoon conform more closely to the reformers' aesthetic ideals. The vaguely foliate form of the spoon and the strawberries decorating the handles clearly refer to dining. This was an era of specialization, and silverware, in particular, took on distinct forms for distinct tasks. Serving spoons were often decorated with fruit motifs and were intended for berries or fruit desserts. The bowls of the spoons were often gilded to counteract the effects of the fruit's acid on silver. Berry spoons were often sold separately from sets of flatware, making them common and appropriate wedding gifts.

Sterling silver wheelbarrow, English, c. 1860
COLLECTION LANCENE LOWELL UNION
Sterling silver serving pieces, English, c. 1880
COLLECTION LANCENE LOWELL UNION

THE TIFFANY TOUCH

Tiffany and Company, now world-famous as a jeweler and purveyor of luxury goods, was founded in New York in 1837 as Tiffany, Young, and Ellis. The store sold primarily decorative objects imported from Europe or the Far East, but soon expanded its range to include silver and jewelry. Some objects were made by Tiffany craftsmen and some, like this fruit stand, were crafted independently and retailed by Tiffany.

In the Victorian era, as now, the Tiffany name was associated with extremely high-quality materials, design, and craftsmanship. These two objects, though stylistically dissimilar, both exhibit classic Tiffany characteristics. The fruit stand, manufactured in 1866, is Renaissance revival in style—Tiffany did a great deal of work in various revival styles. The stern masks, the serpent swags, the handles formed from female bodies, are all carefully modeled in meticulous and ornate detail.

The pitcher is just as carefully crafted, with very realistic-looking bas-relief fish, engraved weeds, and curious feet in the form of aquatic vegetation. This is not a revival piece. Instead, early Japanese influence appears in the simple geometric band around the pitcher's top and the asymmetrical placement of the fish on the body of the pitcher.

Sterling silver pitcher, Tiffany and Co., New York, c. 1870
HOFFMAN-GAMPETRO ANTIQUES
Sterling silver fruit stand, Tiffany and Co., New York, 1866
PRIVATE COLLECTION

Silver plate covered vegetable dish,
probably English, late 19th century
SOOKY GOODFRIEND II GALLERY
Silver plate cream and sugar set, probably American, late 19th century
COLLECTION KATHRYN LICHTER

PLATED WARES

The development of electroplating techniques brought a version of silver within the reach of many more consumers in the nineteenth century. The process laid a thin coating of silver over a base of either nickel or copper alloy. Because Sheffield, England, was a great center for this kind of metalwork, items made this way are frequently known as "Sheffield plate." (Often these items are labeled "EPNS," for English Plated Nickel Silver.)

The technique was especially popular for large objects such as trays, candelabras, and vegetable dishes like this one, all of which would have been prohibitively expensive in sterling.

The dish's design is a Victorian hybrid. The chaste rectangular shape, applied shield, and gadroon border hark back to the eighteenth century. But the naturalistic handle in the form of entwined twigs (which could be removed, making the cover a separate dish) is strictly Victorian.

This twig motif, charming to our eyes, was the sort of detail that irritated Charles Eastlake and other design reformers. In *Hints on Household Taste,* Eastlake states that, "A simple ring or round knob would be an infinitely better handle for dish-covers, &c., than the twisted stalks, gilt acorns, sea-shells, and other silly inventions which we find so constantly repeated on them."

Eastlake would probably also have disapproved of the cream and sugar set, which exhibits an almost dizzying variety of decorations. But it was precisely this kind of exuberant ornateness that the middle class appreciated in their first pieces of silver plate. After all, what was the point of having the stuff if it didn't look expensive?

THE PITCHER OF GOOD CHEER

Toby jugs like this were one of the early products of small Staffordshire potteries. They began appearing in the early eighteenth century, though no one knows who invented the form. Nor does anyone know exactly who "Toby" was, though there are a few possibilities.

In those days, highwaymen (who held up carriages on lonely roads) were called "High Tobies" and their colleagues in crime, footpads (muggers, basically), were known as "Low Tobies." Another possible namesake was a Yorkshireman named Henry Elwes, otherwise famous as "Toby Fillpot," who was reputed to have drunk some two thousand gallons of ale in his lifetime.

The Toby Fillpot theory seems likely, since the early Toby jugs, at about ten inches high, would have held a goodly amount of brew. These Tobies were dressed in typical eighteenth-century costume: knee breeches, waistcoat, long coat, and tricorn hat, which served as the jug's spout. They were usually naturalistically colored and glazed.

Toby jugs began to be manufactured in great numbers from about 1840, and variations soon appeared. They are now turned out by the big potters like Doulton and Spode, in forms ranging from Santa Claus to Winston Churchill to Falstaff. The modern Tobies are often formed from the face alone, but this rotund late nineteenth-century Toby is shaped more like a pitcher than a person. It's impossible to make out who he is, since he seems to be robed as a monk. But monks didn't wear tricorn hats. Nor did monks (in the popular imagination, anyway) exhibit the kind of bibulous good cheer visible on this fellow's face.

Earthenware Toby jug, English, c. 1850-75
SOOKY GOODFRIEND II GALLERY

Sterling silver and glass decanter,
American, 1892
COLLECTION LANCENE LOWELL UNION
Silver plate decanter, French, c. 1890;
Cut crystal champagne glasses,
American, late 19th century
HOFFMAN-GAMPETRO ANTIQUES

CHEERS

Fine red wines are usually poured from the bottle into a decanter to aerate the wine and improve its bouquet, and to ensure that the sediment, or "lees," stays in the bottle. In even middle-class houses a century ago, white wines received the same treatment, so decanters were standard and frequently used household equipment.

This handsome silver and glass decanter was a trophy. A panel in the floral design reads, "W.C. Buchanan, First Prize Handicap Pool Tournament, Union League Club, 1892." Its rounded shape and the floral pierced silver mounted over glass hark back to a style that was popular in the late seventeenth century.

The plain silver decanter, shaped like a conventional wine bottle, is a simpler example rendered in silver plate. The cut crystal champagne glasses next to it are in the saucer shape that is quite familiar to us. This shape came into fashion, however, only after some glasses of this form were displayed at London's Great Exhibition in 1851. Legend (probably unknown to the prudish Victorians) has it that the shallow bowl was modeled after a woman's breast.

THE OLD BISCUIT BARREL

The middle-class Victorian table had a lot more on it than the middle-class modern table, and the biscuit barrel was almost as common as the caster set (see page 81). These barrels were used to serve biscuits or crackers at any meal. The shape is a rather witty allusion to the big wooden barrels used to stock biscuits and other staples in general stores.

Even after the gradual rise of national food brands later in the nineteenth century, no food would have been served directly from the package. In genteel circles it would have been considered extremely gauche to put a biscuit tin on the table, attractive though the tin might be (see page 100).

Both the biscuit barrel and the egg and toast rack in the smaller photograph are silver plate. They were thus relatively inexpensive and aimed at genteel rather than outright wealthy customers. The egg and toast rack ingeniously incorporates two pairs of eggcups that can be lifted off and put directly on the plate. Both the rack and the biscuit barrel exhibit one of the most appealing aspects of the Victorian era: a great relish for domestic comfort.

Silver plate and glass biscuit barrel, English, c. 1870
KENTSHIRE GALLERIES
Silver plate egg and toast rack, English, c. 1860
JULIAN GRAHAM-WHITE, LTD.

THE Kitchen

Like most other young matrons,
Meg began her married life with
the determination to be a
model housekeeper.

LOUISA MAY ALCOTT, *Little Women*, 1868

Kitchen, Theodore Sutro Residence, 1899
320 West 102nd Street, New York City
Museum of the City of New York
The Byron Collection
Background wallpaper design: Schumacher

*T*he room in the Victorian house that was the least affected by fashion was the kitchen. It was a strictly utilitarian spot, devoted to the most labor-intensive portions of the housewife's duties: feeding her household, washing the dishes, and doing the laundry. Kitchens were always on the ground floor, and in all but the most modest of houses, they were separated from the more formal rooms. Proximity to the dining room was not considered essential. In fact, the Victorian householder had such a dread of cooking smells permeating the front of the house that "modern" designs for houses included corridors with several sharp angles and doors to keep the odors where they belonged. Ideally, a kitchen would have a high ceiling and lots of windows to provide ample light and ventilation, and it always had a door to the outside, so that food could be delivered directly without going through the front of the house.

Furnishings were kept simple. Most kitchens featured a central work table, usually with a wooden top. It could be used for food preparation as well as serving informal meals for servants or family. A wide dresser for storing china was also common. This was not a chest of drawers, but what is now sometimes called a hutch: a tall piece of furniture with drawers or cupboards below waist level and tall shallow shelves above for displaying plates.

Other furnishings depended on the household. In a midwestern farmer's house, the kitchen was also the laundry room, sewing room, nursery, and family room. There might be a comfortable chair or two, possibly a rag rug in front of the stove, and all the evidence of family life, such as a sewing basket, schoolbooks, and a chromolithographed calendar nailed to the wall. Prosperous urban kitchens, however, might be all business, containing nothing more decorative or cozy than tea towels hung up to dry.

If there wasn't a separate scullery, the deep sink, used for washing vegetables and pots, stood along one wall with a drying rack alongside. Pots were usually hung from the walls or from sturdy racks suspended from the ceiling. Dishes were washed in large bowls, sometimes tin, sometimes wooden, because wood was easier on fine porcelain.

The kitchen was dominated, naturally enough, by the stove. Most of us have a cozy image of a shiny, solid black range fitted with features such as grills and warming shelves. In fact, the average stove was something of a monster. To begin with, it wasn't insulated as today's stoves are, but gave off a great deal of heat. It was also temperamental. Oven heat varied according to the amount of coal that had just been fed into the belly of the stove. The best way to gauge the temperature of an oven was to sprinkle a pinch of flour into it and see what shade of brown it turned. To top it all off, coal ranges had to be meticulously cleaned, the flues scraped out daily with special brushes, and the surface refurbished with a brushing of a substance called "black lead."

Surprisingly enough, housewives didn't rush to embrace gas ranges when they appeared in the middle of the century. The general suspicion about gas (gas lamps, for instance, caused illness if they were snuffed out rather than being turned off) carried over to cooking. Gas was thought to leave noxious residues in food. It was not until the turn of the century that the insulated, clean, easily-controlled gas stoves that we know today began to replace their coal-burning predecessors.

As Napoleon could always manage to assemble his troops on a given spot at a given time, from whatever distance they might have been drawn, so the cook, with a good head for business, can contrive that all her dishes shall be ready.

J. H. WALSH, *Manual of Domestic Economy,* 1857

If the stoves weren't difficult enough, Victorian methods of storing food can dispel any of our lingering culinary nostalgia. Keeping things cold meant ice, period. It could be bought year-round in large chunks and placed in insulated ice chests. Some larger houses might have a spring house or a cool pantry, perhaps even a dairy where marble counters and heavy walls kept butter and milk cool. Fish was stored with chipped ice and eaten soon after being caught. Meat, however, was stored at room temperature in a cage-like screened contraption known as a "meat safe." It did keep meat safe from vermin and flies, but didn't do much to keep it from spoiling.

Vermin, whether insect or mammal, were a constant nuisance. Closed cupboards were often avoided in kitchens precisely because they made such lovely homes for mice or cockroaches, while dry goods such as flour, sugar, cornmeal, and spices all had to be stored in pottery or wooden containers.

Of course, the sure way to keep the population of vermin down is constant cleaning. Different substances required different cleaning methods. Wood, since it absorbs flavors, was scrubbed with sand and water. Copper—which was very popular for saucepans and jelly molds—was usually polished with fine sand and soft soap until it gleamed. Stainless steel had not been invented, so knife blades were scoured with brick dust and polished on a scrap of carpet.

And there were lots of dishes. Even the most modest family was larger in those days, and servants, if there were any, had to be fed. Meals, too, were more elaborate. Middle-class families might not attempt fashionable French dishes, but an 1897 etiquette book aimed at the middle class says, "Soup, fish, *entrée*, joint, game, sweet, savoury, suffice to any man."

In the ambitious kitchen, no dish went to the dining room without its little decorations of boiled egg, truffle, beet, parsley, or olive. In fact, one of the great culinary urges of the era was to make food resemble something else. One of the most popular dishes was the galantine, a labor-intensive dish in which a loin of pork or veal is disassembled, stuffed with forcemeat, eggs, truffles, and olives, trussed into a cloth, boiled in broth, weighted and chilled, then sliced and served with chopped jellied aspic.

Two other staples of the period, ice cream and jellies, are still served today, but the Victorians made them into elaborate structures using copper molds. Jellies were often studded with fresh fruits and ice cream was often layered into bombe molds, so called because they looked like explosive ordnance. The *trompe l'oeil* instinct was so strong that in kitchens capable of it, ice-cream bombes were served surrounded by spun-sugar "flames."

That kind of elaborate cookery is as out of date now as the calling card; it clearly belongs to a life that was radically different from ours. So, in truth, does the nostalgic image of a warm family group gathered around a kitchen table by the light of an oil lamp. But today's romanticized notion of the middle-class Victorian kitchen continues to beguile us with an image of warmth, stability, and something savory bubbling on the back of the stove.

Three yellow ware bowls, American, late 19th century
COLLECTION KATHRYN LICHTER

MIX AND MATCH

The various names for ceramics have historically been used so loosely that the terms "pottery" and "china" sometimes overlap. In fact, they describe a range of items from translucent bone china to sturdy stoneware. What they all have in common is that they are manufactured from clay. Their correct names refer to the composition of the basic material and the method of manufacture.

These mixing bowls are a kind of earthenware called yellow ware. The name comes from the color of the clay, which was quite common in the mid-Atlantic and midwestern states. Although, traditionally, bowls like this would have been thrown by hand on a pottery wheel, pressing or pouring wet clay into molds allowed manufacturers to produce uniform goods more quickly. Yellow ware was produced into the 1900s, much of it molded. It was fired twice, once to dry the clay, then again to set the clear glaze that was usually applied to it. (The simple bands on these bowls are characteristic of yellow ware mixing bowls: they were usually made of slip, or liquid clay, painted on before the second firing.)

Bowls like this were a staple of every American kitchen. An 1896 catalog from a Syracuse pottery company offers them in "yellow" (as seen here) or "Rockingham," which was a brown glaze. They came in ten sizes, from three gallons down to three-quarters of a pint. The smallest cost only forty cents the dozen.

TOOLS OF THE TRADE

The foods that come out of the kitchen today are quite different from what they were a hundred years ago. Many of our ingredients and techniques would seem bizarre to Victorian cooks. But some of the relics of the era would fit seamlessly into our kitchens today.

The Even-Full mixer is a sensible contraption, something between an egg-beater and a blender. It would have come in handy for whipping cream, beating eggs, or making mayonnaise, all of which were central tasks given the complex, sauce-laden style of Victorian cuisine.

This rolling pin, stoneware with maple handles, clearly means business. Some cooks today still opt for a ceramic pin like this because it can be chilled to facilitate working with buttery pastry on a hot day.

The whimsical milk glass jars and the small stoneware jar probably served to store small amounts of condiments or spices. The screw-top jars were ideal for keeping expensive spices fresh. The stoneware pot belongs to a type known as "herb pots," though it could have served a multitude of uses. This jar features the typical blue slip underglaze decoration and nubby saltglazed finish so often found on stoneware.

The milk thermometers in the inset picture are all filled with real mercury, which makes them handsome, if dangerous (mercury is poisonous). Cooks know that if milk boils it forms a nasty skin as it cools, so these thermometers may have been used for delicate sauces or puddings. Or they might have been intended to test the temperature of milk for a baby's bottle. Although most women nursed if possible, some babies were given milk from bottles with rubber nipples, just as they are today.

Glass and metal Even-Full mixer; Stoneware and maple rolling pin; Milk glass jars with metal tops; Stoneware herb pot, American, late 19th century
PROPOSITION RENTALS
Glass and mercury milk thermometers, late 19th century
YALE R. BURGE ANTIQUES

Tin biscuit boxes, English, 1880s and 1890s
PRIVATE COLLECTION

TOP TINS

One of the striking changes that took place in the late Victorian era was the packaging and marketing of individual brands of groceries. Through much of the century, general stores supplied the needs of a local circle of customers. Staples like flour, salt, and sugar were displayed in large barrels or tins and were sold by weight.

This practice gradually shifted as gigantic food processing companies such as Quaker Oats began producing standard packages of foodstuffs, thus ensuring consistent quality from purchase to purchase. The National Biscuit Company (forerunner of Nabisco) brought out Uneeda Biscuits in 1898. These soda crackers in their patented airtight boxes presented tremendous competition for the cracker barrels that had been basic to every general store.

Some companies wisely made their packaging a selling point. These colorful tins from England contained Huntley & Palmer's biscuits ("cookies" in American usage). The "Artist's Palette" box dates from 1900, and was the first in a line of increasingly whimsical shapes. Many of the twentieth-century biscuit tins had moving parts and ended their useful days as children's toys long after the biscuits had been consumed.

Engaging as these tins are, they would not have appeared on the dining room table. Cookies and crackers would be served from a a plate or a biscuit barrel like the one on page 93.

KITCHEN GOLD

Simple pottery articles for the kitchen were usually quite plain, but late in the century the technique of sponging came into fashion. Items made of earthenware, stoneware, or ironstone were glazed in a pale color, usually white or yellow. A darker color was then applied with a sponge in a loose freehand pattern. The most common colors are blue, green, gray, tan, and brown, and sometimes two or three colors are combined.

Since the sponging technique didn't become widespread until around 1890, most spongeware is molded rather than thrown on a wheel. The two bowls here were formed in molds with decoratively shaped lips; there is also some decoration around the foot of the smaller bowl. The lips, and the lip of the taller jar, have been gilded. There is actually an unusual amount of gilding still adhering to these bowls, probably because the lips received little wear.

Spongeware bowls, pitcher, and jar, American, after 1890
COLLECTION KATHRYN LICHTER

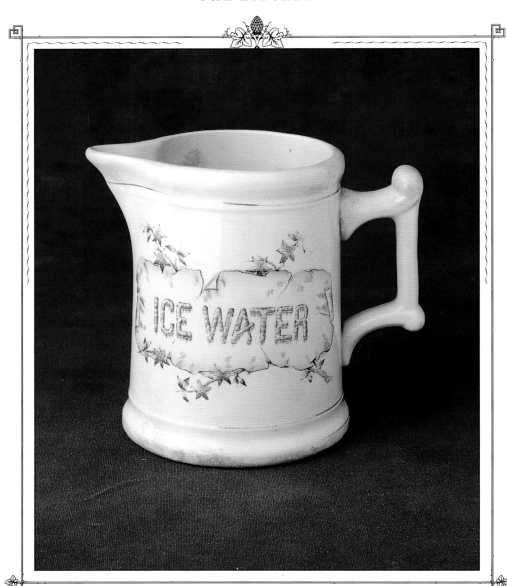

Earthenware pitcher, American, c. 1890
COLLECTION JOYCE BALDWIN

THE ICEMAN COMETH

Americans who have spent any time in Europe drinking lukewarm beer and paying for glasses of water often come home with a new appreciation for something we usually take for granted: ice water. (Ours is the only modern nation that could conceive of refrigerators that dispense the stuff from panels in the doors.)

This is not a new phenomenon. In most of the continental U.S., we're exposed to extremes of temperature. In very cold weather, everything freezes, including waterways. In very hot weather, we use chunks of that ice to cool ourselves off. European visitors have continuously been taken aback by this custom. Many English tourists published their impressions when they got home from America, and on this issue they often sound like George Makepeace Towle, who wrote, in 1870, "There is ice everywhere; ice in the great metallic 'pitcher' on the breakfast and dinner table, ice on the butter, ice on the radishes, ice for the meat and fish in the cellar, ice for the beverages—the water and claret and punch. . . ."

This sturdy earthenware pitcher might have been used in a kitchen or a hotel. Its transfer-printed label (apparently peeling off in a whimsical bit of late-Victorian *trompe l'oeil*) bears the words "Ice Water" in dripping icicle letters.

COOL, MAN

This heavy crockery jug is the Victorian version of the office water cooler. Cool, clean, drinkable water from a tap was not something to be relied on even a hundred years ago.

The "XXth Century" trademark blazoned on the front of this cooler is probably a bit of futuristic marketing hyperbole, and indeed, this cooler does look quite different from earlier examples of the genre. Coolers were widely produced from the late eighteenth century onward, in several kinds of earthenware (spongeware, stoneware, yellow earthenware). Although some were quite complex, the usual form was a simple barrel shape with a stoppered hole at the bottom. The idea was elementary: water or other beverages were poured in with ice to keep them cold. The cooler could be kept in the kitchen or lugged outside to quench the thirst of men working in the fields.

The XXth Century version has a matching cover and a metal spigot, characteristics that set it apart from its XIXth Century predecessors. Its wide-bottomed shape would make it very difficult to tip over, which was surely an improvement on the classic narrow-bottomed barrel shape.

Earthenware water cooler,
Gordley & Hayes, New York, c. 1900
COLLECTION CECILY BARTH FIRESTEIN

Glazed stoneware crocks, late 19th century
PROPOSITION RENTALS

WHAT A CROCK

Since most groceries were sold in bulk a hundred years ago, the average Victorian kitchen was stocked with more storage containers than we have today. They ranged from wooden boxes to tin meatsafes, from stoneware jugs to china canisters. Crocks like these were especially handy all-purpose containers.

Their exact use is a matter of conjecture, of course. Although they are usually known as crocks today, crocks smaller than six inches tall were usually called cake pots by their manufacturers. Larger crocks were known as butter pots, although they were often used for pickling vegetables. Similarly shaped crocks also came in huge sizes that held as much as fifty gallons; these were called meat tubs.

Most straight-sided crocks like these were made of stoneware, an extremely durable earthenware that was fired at a very high temperature until the clay became vitreous. It wasn't until late in the nineteenth century that potteries developed molding machines for stoneware. These crocks, with their panels of rococo-style swags and curlicues, were obviously molded. Traditionally, such stoneware was decorated with dark blue slip (liquid clay) and was saltglazed, which produced a distinctive, slightly bumpy surface. Although these crocks have not been saltglazed (the texture would have interfered with the molded ornament), the transparent wash of blue on their lids and bodies conforms to the traditional color scheme for stoneware.

BEAUTY IS AS BEAUTY DOES

William Morris once summed up his home design credo by saying, "Have nothing in your house that you do not know to be useful, or believe to be beautiful." One of the most appealing characteristics of the Victorian age is that utility and beauty so often go hand in hand. Of course many ugly and useless things were made (and are often found for sale in antique stores). But they are far outnumbered by handsome, practical objects such as the acorn-shaped brass coal scuttle on page 45, the engaging ribbon-tied chamber pot on page 132, or these beautifully detailed kitchen tools.

These were all gadgets from well-to-do homes, because (with the exception of the ice crusher) they are made of sterling silver. On the left are grape shears, used to cut a small cluster of grapes from a bunch. The central item with the wooden handle and engraved diamond-shaped blade is something of a mystery, though the shape of the blade suggests that it could be used for both cutting and serving. (A cheese knife seems a logical possibility.) Next are sugar tongs, for picking up small lumps of sugar (sugar was sold in large, hard loaves in those days). The horn handle of the ice crusher permits a firm grip, which was necessary. Ice was purchased in blocks, and every kitchen contained picks, shavers, and crushers to pummel it into the appropriate size and form.

The spoon holder in the inset photograph would have made a stylish addition to a tea tray. The peacock feather was an extremely popular motif in the late nineteenth century, taken up first in advanced "Aesthetic" circles and gradually trickling down to the middle-class kitchen.

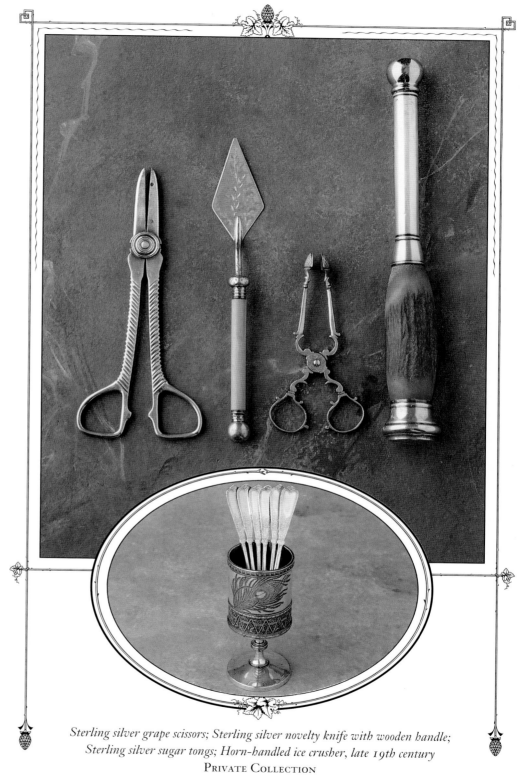

Sterling silver grape scissors; Sterling silver novelty knife with wooden handle; Sterling silver sugar tongs; Horn-handled ice crusher, late 19th century
PRIVATE COLLECTION
Silver plate spoon holder with silver plate spoons, late 19th century
PRIVATE COLLECTION

Glass rolling pin, English, late 19th century
PRIVATE COLLECTION

ROLY-POLY

This vividly striped object looks far too exotic to be functional, but it is in fact a rolling pin.

Rolling pins, surprisingly enough, have a long history as decorative objects. From the late Middle Ages, they were made out of pottery. Starting in the seventeenth century, these pottery pins were enlivened with underglaze decorations: mottoes, flowers, dates, and names. They were often given as mementos of christenings and weddings. They were also given as love tokens, a notion that seems extremely unromantic today. Some more prosaic versions were hollow and were used as holding containers for sugar or salt, or even smaller cooking tools.

This florid pattern in two shades of glass is known as "Nailsea," for the glassworks in the west of England that pioneered the style, but probably only a small percentage of this work was actually produced at the Nailsea factory. It is also sometimes called "end-of-day glass," because workers used whatever glass was left at the end of the day to create novelty items that their families could sell for a little bit of extra income.

FARM CHARM

These two modest pieces of earthenware illustrate two rather different approaches to ornament. The plate is quite simple in form, though the figures on its rim are molded and raised, then painted by hand in shades of red and blue. The placid bovine in the center of the dish, however, is transfer printed.

This technique involved applying transfers (designs on paper) to pieces that were about to go into the kiln. The paper burned away in the heat of the firing, leaving the colored design on the surface of the piece. Glaze was applied afterward.

Transfer-printed motifs are often rather static and regular, even mechanical looking, but they could give effects of shading and detail that were very expensive to render freehand. The technique was often combined with handpainting, much as mechanically produced engravings intended for parlor walls were often hand-tinted. (The compote on page 76 is another example of transfer-printed ware.)

The covered dish in the smaller photograph is another molded piece, and it looks as if the designer was all but intoxicated by the decorative possibilities of this technique. The dish features shells, scrolls, and fluting, branches with leaves and cherries, a twig-shaped handle on the lid (one of Charles Eastlake's pet peeves; see page 90) and two applied handles formed of animal heads, though a biologist might be hard put to make an exact identification. The enthusiastic combination of motifs is characteristic of the style known loosely as "Rococo Revival." Probably what saves it, to the modern eye, is that it has an unadorned matte finish.

Earthenware dish, English, late 19th century
COLLECTION JUDY SINGER
Covered earthenware dish with plate, English, c. 1860
COLLECTION JUDY SINGER

Glazed pottery bowl, probably English, c. 1890
HOFFMAN-GAMPETRO ANTIQUES
Wooden breadboard and wood and steel bread knife, late 19th century
COLLECTION CECILY BARTH FIRESTEIN

BREAD AND BOARD

This blue bowl, with its incised decoration, shows the widespread influence of the Arts and Crafts movement. The stylized lilies below the rim are typical of the abstracted natural images popular among followers of William Morris. Furthermore, both the decoration and the shape, with smooth interior and heavy built-up rim, indicate that this bowl was pressed or poured in a mold, rather than having been hand-thrown on a wheel. This contrasts with the yellow ware bowls on page 98, which, though they were probably not hand-thrown, maintain the smooth gradual slant, turned lip, and stripes that hark back to the potter's wheel.

This bowl is ten and a half inches wide at the rim, a handy size for leaving bread dough to rise on the back of the stove. Breadmaking was one of the routine tasks of any Victorian kitchen. Although commercial bakeries began to be established at the middle of the century, as late as 1900, more than three-quarters of Americans still baked their bread at home. This was a matter of pride for most housewives, and even if they had daily help they might do the baking (of cakes, pies, brown and white breads) themselves. The process, from proofing the yeast to baking, took about twenty-four hours.

Since wood absorbs flavors so easily, it made sense to reserve a special cutting board for bread. The appropriate knife, like the specialty knives on page 117, says on the handle what it is to be used for. Round breadboards and knives like this were often sold together as a set.

ARTSY CRAFTSY

A constant theme in the decorative arts after about 1870 was the relationship between aesthetics and machines. The negative effects of the industrial age were becoming apparent. To some observers, it seemed that many of society's ills could be righted by a return to simpler, cleaner manual labor. At the very least, one could furnish one's house with honest, handmade objects.

The Arts and Crafts movement that held this philosophy produced objects with a distinctive look. Although they do not look modern in the way that some of Christopher Dresser's designs do (see pages 84 and 85), neither do they look as obviously "Victorian" as, for example, the covered dish on page 107. In spite of the fact that they were produced during the height of the Victorian era, this copper vase and candlesticks look as if they might have been made anytime in the last hundred years.

Arts and Crafts-style objects like these were often produced in small workshops founded to "improve" the lives of honest workers. The vase is the product of the Yattendon Metalworking Class, founded by Mrs. Alfred Waterhouse (wife of a famous architect) to keep the men of her village off the streets at night. Mrs. Waterhouse provided the designs and materials, and the men were paid for their pieces that sold.

The candlesticks come from the Newlyn School of the Applied Arts. This was founded by painter J. D. Mackenzie in a Cornwall fishing village to provide fishermen with an alternate source of income. Like many Newlyn pieces, these candlesticks are decorated with fish and marine flora.

Copper vase, Yattendon, England, c. 1895
KURLAND • ZABAR GALLERY
Copper candlesticks, Newlyn, England, c. 1895
KURLAND • ZABAR GALLERY

Brass trivets, mid to late 19th century
SOOKY GOODFRIEND II GALLERY

TOP BRASS

When you put a hot pot or dish down on wood, it can seriously damage the finish or the wood itself. In the mid-nineteenth century, when varnished or "French-polished" furniture was very popular, a perfectly glassy finish was considered the height of elegance.

Marking the surface of a table was a great concern, and most households would possess one or more trivets like these. Brass, which is an alloy of copper and zinc, was the ideal metal for trivets and hot plates because it could be polished to an attractive glow, but didn't conduct heat.

The two shown here might each have been used for slightly different purposes. The round trivet, with its wooden handle and iron legs, could have served to keep a pot warm near the fire. The iron legs would not easily be marked by the heat, or show smears of coal or ash. The pot on it would stay warm without being blackened by the flames.

The square trivet, with its turned pedestal, was more likely to be used on top of a table. In the 1840s, stands like these came with matching brass teakettles, and the simple pierced ornamentation of this trivet suggests that it may date from mid-century.

DOG DAYS

One of the most popular uses for papier-mâché was the manufacture of large, ornately shaped serving trays like this one. The malleable nature of the medium and its light weight made it very practical for this purpose, and the large flat surface afforded by the tray was an ideal decorative opportunity.

This tray is a classic example of the mid-Victorian genre. Its curving outline, gold-scrolled borders, and dog painting are typical characteristics. Many such trays, in fact, are decorated with copies of dog paintings by Sir Edwin Landseer.

Landseer, a favorite painter of Queen Victoria's, specialized in two areas: Highland themes (many of which featured deer, either dead or alive) and dogs. Landseer's dog paintings succeed in capturing both the physical and the temperamental idiosyncrasies of the breeds he pictured.

This pop-eyed brown and white spaniel is rather more crudely painted than anything from Landseer's brush. It is probably a King Charles spaniel, a highly bred variety of dog that was popular for its "aristocratic" connections. This spaniel is wearing a pretty pearl-trimmed collar and also has pierced ears. The Victorians were much given to anthropomorphizing their pets, and decking a beloved canine in jewels may have seemed perfectly appropriate. The earrings may be a further reference to swashbuckling Stuart courtiers, many of whom (both male and female) had pierced ears.

Papier-mâché tray, English, c. 1850
JULIAN GRAHAM-WHITE, LTD.

Cast-iron hand-cranked sewing machine,
American, c. 1860
E. BUK
Crazy quilt pincushion filled with emery, late 19th century
LAURA FISHER

STITCHES IN TIME

The invention of the sewing machine in the early 1850s had tremendous social repercussions, culminating in the eventual development of the ready-to-wear clothing industry. It had an impact on the average household as well, since most middle-class Americans continued to wear clothes that were made at home even after commercially manufactured garments became available in stores. In Laura Ingalls Wilder's *These Happy Golden Years*, Ma praises the new machine, saying, "It does the work so easily; tucking is no trouble at all. And such beautiful stitching. The best of seamstresses could not possibly equal it by hand."

That was it in a nutshell: the sewing machine simply did the job better and faster. Some fashion historians have even proposed that the elaborately constructed fashions of the 1870s, with their fringes and pleating and gathering and yard upon yard of trim, were a response to the new possibilities made available to the dressmaker. Certainly sewing machines made better clothes possible farther down the economic scale.

As well as being useful, sewing machines were decorative. They were not styled, as they are today, to stress function alone. This hand-cranked cast-iron model, only six inches high, is beautified by graceful scrolling lines and a rose hand-painted on the bottom plate.

The pincushion in the smaller picture exhibits the same Victorian trait of making practicality attractive. It is stitched in the classic "crazy quilt" pattern, using up odd scraps of fabric. The cushion is full of emery, a sandlike mineral powder used to keep pins and needles sharp.

Ironbound

Ironing was an inevitable chore in the nineteenth century, when large families and no synthetic fabrics meant piles of shirts and underclothes, sheets and tablecloths that had to be pressed flat every time they were washed. Merely setting up for the task was a tremendous production.

First, the folding ironing board wasn't widely available until the 1890s, so most housekeepers used one of several different sized boards, padded and covered with muslin, propped between the kitchen table and a chair.

Irons came in a wide variety. Box irons had a compartment that could be filled with coals, while slug irons like this one held a piece of metal that had been heated on the stove. But the most common was the flatiron, also known as a sadiron. ("Sad," in this case, being a synonym for "heavy.") Equipped with a detachable handle of wood, the whole flatiron was heated (repeatedly) for use.

A housewife might use as many as three flatirons at a time. While one was in use, the other two would be heating up on the stove. They were available in different weights and sizes for different jobs: polishing a highly starched shirt front required a round edge, while getting the wrinkles out of a damask tablecloth demanded a heavy iron.

Of course if you put a hot iron face down on any surface for long it will leave a big scorch mark. These handsome brass shield-shaped trivets were the answer to that problem. They probably date from the middle of the century, because the "stands" that were sold with irons by the 1880s usually had a lip at the point to keep the iron from sliding off. Some stands or trivets were decorative like these, while more promotional items had the name of the manufacturer pressed into them.

Brass slug iron with wood handle, mid-19th century
E. Buk
Brass trivets, mid-19th century
Sooky Goodfriend II Gallery

Graniteware double boiler and muffin tin, American, late 19th century
PRIVATE COLLECTION

GIVE THEM GRANITE

Among the exhibits at the Philadelphia Centennial Exposition of 1876 was a new kind of kitchenware that was described as "light, elegant, clean, and everlasting." It was called, variously, graniteware, agate ware, enamelware, and glazed ware, names that describe its innovative feature: a sturdy glaze of enamel that would liberate housewives from scouring cast iron or polishing copper.

Graniteware was an instant success, and has, in various forms, been manufactured ever since. Although enamel is brittle and pieces can chip if they are roughly handled, enameled metal is an extremely practical material. It doesn't react with acidic foods the way some metals do. It is heat-proof and easy to clean. And it can be produced in any color or pattern.

One of the most familiar patterns of graniteware is the swirl, seen here on the muffin tin and double boiler. This pattern is still being produced today, frequently in the traditional dark blue and white colors. Other common colors were gray, brown, light blue, green, and turquoise, and they were no doubt a welcome bit of brightness in the utilitarian world of cookware. Mottling, as seen on the teapots opposite, was another extremely common pattern, and pieces could be enameled with words or pictures as well.

True Blue Enameled Ware Patent Seamless Milk or Rice Boilers, with enameled cover to fit both vessels.

No.	Quarts inside Boiler	Holds Quarts	Price, Each.
52	1	1½	$0.82
53	2	1⅞	1.06
54	3	3	1.37
56	4	4½	1.55

TIP ME OVER AND POUR ME OUT

One of the beauties of graniteware was that it was so adaptable. Soon after its 1876 invention, companies all over the American east and midwest were turning out everything from chamber pots to cruet stands in enameled metal. You could set your table with it. You could furnish your bathroom with it. You could cook every course of every meal with it, then serve the meal and wash up afterward using only graniteware. The stuff was sturdy, attractive, and cheap.

There were also attempts to make it a little more genteel. Most graniteware pieces are not ornamented; the bold enamel itself provides the decoration on items like ladles and pie plates and saucepans. That was to be expected when prices were low (a three-quart pitcher, for instance, was listed for forty-two cents in the fall 1900 Sears catalog).

But some pieces, like these tea- and coffeepots, were more carefully made. Enamel might be laid on in two or three or more coats to give a more durable finish, and sometimes three colors were used. Different metals were used for trimming, as in all of the pots here, and the trimming took on some of the ornate decorative motifs of the era. Even the basic shapes, like those of the squat, fluted teapots, could be a bit more elaborate as long as they would still take the essential enamel glaze.

Graniteware coffeepots, American, 1876–1900
PRIVATE COLLECTION
Graniteware teapots, American, 1876–1900
PRIVATE COLLECTION

Cast-iron nutcracker, late 19th century
SOOKY GOODFRIEND II GALLERY

NUT JOB

Twentieth-century ingenuity has yet to come up with an improved nutcracker. The basic principle behind the nutcrackers in use as long ago as the eighteenth century involves placing a nut in some kind of vise and putting enough pressure on it to crush the shell—ideally without also crushing the nut meat.

This cast-iron eagle is an unusual example of a fairly common motif: animal-shaped nutcrackers. A nut would be placed in the jaws of a dog, for instance, or a squirrel, and pressure on the tail would close the jaws. These fancy nutcrackers might be produced in brass as well as cast iron, and might be found in the dining room.

It was traditional in more formal houses for men to linger around the table after dinner. While the ladies drank coffee and chatted in the parlor, men could talk about business, sports, and politics over a glass of port or brandy. Nuts were sometimes served as an accompaniment to the spirits. Individual silver-plated nutcrackers shaped like pliers might even be provided.

More utilitarian-looking crackers were manufactured for kitchen use, including several models that could be clamped onto a table. None of them, however, sped up the fiddly, tedious task of removing nut meats from mangled shells. A pecan pie, in the days before preshelled nuts, was clearly quite a labor-intensive proposition.

SO SPECIAL

These days, "all-purpose" is an appealing notion. One item that can perform four different tasks saves time, space, and money. This is a point of view completely alien to the Victorian age, when people took positive delight in things that served only one purpose. This book is full of objects that have single, often arcane, uses (like the spoon warmer on page 79).

The mania for specialization wasn't limited to the upper classes. Utensils like these are quite common in antique stores, and they are sometimes made of modest materials like silver plate or nickel with wooden handles, usually labeled with their intended use. Perhaps it gave less wealthy householders a feeling of prosperity to own a fork that was consecrated to pickles alone.

The fork on the far right, with waisted handle and small tines, is the pickle fork. Pickles were a common condiment on the Victorian table, especially in middle-class families that couldn't afford fresh vegetables out of season. The fork with the fish engraved just below the tines is a sardine fork. Sardines were considered quite a treat a hundred years ago. The two broad-bladed knives are for butter; one proclaims this on the handle, one on the blade. The knife on the far left, has a serrated edge for cutting the stubborn skins of lemons.

Sterling silver and silver plate forks and knives with wooden and bone handles, late 19th century
COLLECTION JUDY SINGER

Cast-iron and wood coffee mill, American, after 1876
PRIVATE COLLECTION

JAVA JIVE

The great minds that labored hard to reduce the Victorian housewife's burden did not manage to come up with a way to abbreviate the coffee-making process. In most Victorian homes, making a cup of coffee was a complex task that surpasses even what today's most finicky coffee snob goes through for his daily ration of caffeine.

To begin with, many households roasted their own coffee. Today's commercial roasters inform us that this is an amazingly delicate task, requiring the most sophisticated equipment and skilled workers. A hundred years ago, coffee beans were roasted in the oven to meet each day's needs.

Beans, naturally, were also ground at home, and though coffee mills came in many different sizes and shapes, they generally worked the same way. Beans were poured into a hopper, a handle was cranked, the beans passed between opposing burrs, and the ground coffee fell into a drawer or dish.

This cast-iron mill was manufactured by the Enterprise company and bears a seal proclaiming that it was exhibited at the Philadelphia Centennial Exposition in 1876. The same model was still being offered by the Biddle Hardware Company Catalog in 1910, so we can assume it had proven a successful item. The hopper held four ounces of coffee, and the catalog claims that it ground six ounces in one minute (they can't have allowed for refilling the hopper). In 1910, the mill cost $2.25, which was fairly expensive. The cheapest model, a wooden box with a tin hopper, cost $4.00 per dozen wholesale.

HAVE WE GOT BANANAS

Even in our utilitarian age, we still devote special dishes or serving implements to very special foods such as caviar or champagne. Bananas, a hundred years ago, were similarly prized, along with pineapples and other tropical fruits. Even native-grown fresh fruit was enough of a treat, in those days before refrigeration, to be served as a separate course at the end of a meal. Tropical fruit was not only especially succulent; it had the additional potent charm of novelty. Newfangled steamships were the first carriers that covered long distances quickly enough to bring foods from the Caribbean to America without spoiling en route.

It's no surprise to see a compote decorated with banana designs made just for that fruit. This kind of raised dish usually gives a food extra prominence and draws diners' attention to it. Bananas might have been displayed on the table throughout the meal and then served—with considerable flourish—for dessert.

Of course, they could not be eaten monkey-style. As one 1902 etiquette book put it, "Bananas are an easy and cleanly fruit to eat at all times. You peel them with your knife and fork, cut them in small pieces, and convey to the mouth on the fork." It's a good deal easier said than done.

Pressed glass banana dish, late 19th century
COLLECTION CECILY BARTH FIRESTEIN

Brass and glass skater's lamp, late 19th century
COLLECTION JOYCE AND CATHERINE BALDWIN

ON THIN ICE

There were not many ways a woman could get physical exercise in the Victorian era, but by the last decade of the nineteenth century health experts were urging women to participate in a growing range of sports. Croquet, lawn tennis, and bicycling were among the popular choices, and skating flourished as well.

Skating required no elaborate equipment as did bicycling, no court as for lawn tennis or croquet, and it offered unparalleled opportunities for flirting. Although Victorian mores seldom permitted courting couples to be alone, it was apparently thought that no harm could come of young people's gliding across the ice hand in hand. It was perfectly acceptable and natural for a young man to help a young lady fasten her skates and support her on the ice. And since nighttime skating parties were a frequent pleasant variation on the theme, a suitor might even be able to snatch a kiss on a dark stretch of ice.

This skater's lamp (about ten inches high) was probably the equivalent of a flashlight under those circumstances. It might have frustrated any amorous designs, but, secured by its chain, with the ring hooked onto a skater's finger, it would certainly have helped its bearer avoid obstacles (sticks, rough spots, or other people) on the ice. The sight of a winter pond by night, with a bonfire glowing on the bank and lights like these gliding by in the dark like fireflies, must have been romantic indeed.

THE WHOLE BALL OF WOOL

Knitters know that it's impossible to knit
with yarn in skeins. The first step in
starting a new project is always rolling
the wool into balls. You can ask your
hired girl or your impatient husband to
hold it for you, or drape it over the posts
of a chair—or use the ingenious swift
reel, manufactured in England, a country
that began producing fine woolens as
early as the Middle Ages.

The manufacture of clothing made
immense strides during the Victorian
era. The invention of the sewing
machine (see page 112) and the subse-
quent development of factories (many of
which produced soldiers' uniforms for
the Civil War) partially relieved women
of the burden of making their menfolks'
shirts or other garments. But socks,
gloves, and mufflers were still knitted at
home. (The time-consuming sweater,
perhaps fortunately for the busy housewife, came into fashion much later.)

Although it was basically utilitarian,
this reel was still handsomely made, especially by the standards of our unadorned
era. The base is carefully shaped and set
on little bun feet, while the brass central
stem is decorated in an elaborate Middle
Eastern pattern and topped with a spired
acorn-shaped finial.

Wood and brass swift reel, English, c. 1870
YALE R. BURGE ANTIQUES

THE Bedroom

*The first requisite in properly performing the
duties of the toilette is to have a regularly-arranged dressing-room.
This room, of course, in many instances, is used as
a bedroom as well; but that need not
interfere with its general arrangements.*

RICHARD A. WELLS,
*Manners Culture and Dress
of the Best American Society,* 1890

*Bedroom, 1904
Museum of the City of New York
The Byron Collection
Background wallpaper design: Schumacher*

*I*n the eighteenth and early nineteenth centuries, aristocratic bedrooms were still quasi-public rooms. They frequently did duty as sitting rooms where guests might be received, so they were decorated with some splendor. By the middle of the nineteenth century, however, the Victorian trend toward specialization was turning bedrooms into chambers offering privacy above all else.

The prudishness that we think of as characteristically Victorian eventually took over so that bedrooms became slightly risqué in some circles. In Edith Wharton's *The Age of Innocence*, set in the 1870s, a fat and elderly matron has rearranged her house so that her bedroom is on the ground floor, visible from the sitting room. "Her visitors were startled and fascinated by the foreignness of this arrangement, which recalled scenes in French fiction, and architectural incentives to immorality."

The mere sight of the bed, with its implication of intimacy, made the dowager's visitors nervous. By mid-century, the old-fashioned fondness for curtained beds was waning, and the new concern with hygiene made housewives look at bed hangings as potential lodging places for dust, bugs, and vermin. Many a family chose to sacrifice the warmth provided by the curtains, and took them down. The wealthy might be tempted by newfangled and sanitary-looking brass or enameled bed frames, or they might instead choose the kind of massive, carved wood head- and footboards that made the bed look like a miniature castle.

The Victorian bed played a crucial role in a marriage. Prudish they might be, but the Victorians did believe in procreation. Given the high rate of childhood mortality, bearing numerous children at least bettered one's chance of raising some to adulthood. And, of course, children were considered, in the mostly Christian attitudes of the age, a blessing from heaven *and* proof of fertility. So the marriage bed as the locus of sexual activity had an immense—albeit unspoken—significance in the bedroom decor.

Additionally, all children were born at home a hundred years ago. A doctor might be present for a difficult delivery, but a midwife more usually helped a woman through an experience that was frightening, painful, and all too often fatal. Women also stayed in bed for several weeks after even the most straightforward childbirth.

The best bedroom in the house—what we think of as the master bedroom—usually also did duty as a sickroom for any family member, adult or child. Because illnesses were often so serious, nursing frequently involved watching over the sickbed day and night, sponging a fevered forehead in lieu of any more efficacious treatment.

In fact, well or ill, children often slept with their parents. Infants were usually breast-fed, and it was simply easier to have them close at hand. Cribs or cradles were often placed next to the parental bed. Older children, too, might well sleep on a trundle bed in their parents' room, though in more prosperous households they would be sent off to sleep in a nursery with a live-in nanny. No doubt these precautions were a reflection of the very high rates of infant mortality.

Most of the activities we now carry out in the bathroom were also relegated to the bedroom. Although fully equipped bathrooms were installed in the homes of the urban wealthy as early as the 1850s, most Victorian families made do with pitchers and bowls of water carried upstairs and placed on mirrored, marble-topped washstands. Washing usually meant a sponge bath with water poured from the pitcher into the washbowl. Total immersion was possible only after elaborate preparations, including transporting water heated in the kitchen to a portable tub, placed usually in the sacrosanct privacy of

As a rule, our modern bedrooms are too fussy in their fittings up.

CHARLES EASTLAKE, *Hints on Household Taste*, 1868

the bedroom. Even late in the century, when bathrooms had become common-place in American middle-class homes, English homes were often inadequately equipped with plumbing. Consuelo Vanderbilt, an American heiress who married an English duke in 1895, grew up in houses with bathrooms and was offended at their absence in her grand new English home.

In houses without plumbing, accommodation also had to be made for the calls of nature. While a visit to an outhouse was feasible during the day, chamber pots were used at night. They were often hidden away in a nightstand next to the bed, or sometimes just tucked beneath the bed for easy access. The contents of the chamber pot were emptied after use into a slops jar, which in turn had to be emptied outdoors in the morning.

The privacy afforded by the bedroom was also important for getting dressed. In the Victorian era, there was very little latitude about how one presented oneself to the world. Deviation in more than minor detail was unthinkable.

Clothing was stored in the bedroom in chests of drawers and wardrobes, as well as in the built-in closets that some houses featured as early as the 1860s. And although middle-class Victorians may not have had as many different outfits as middle-class families do today, day in and day out they wore, quite simply, many more garments.

For example, the new class of managers, the white-collar workers who sat behind desks in offices every day, began by putting on a set of long-sleeved, full-length underwear. Their sober, three-piece wool suits were not unlike what many male professionals wear today, but their highly starched collars were higher and their ties wider. The sight of a man's bare throat was considered very improper until well into the twentieth century.

During the fifty years covered by this book, women's clothing underwent many variations, but one principle never changed: except for the grandest occasions, women were always completely covered up, and with several layers of fabric. (The exception was formal dress which permitted sleeveless, low-cut bodices, and the revelation of this comparatively great expanse of flesh must have been extremely potent.)

Although hoops and bustles came and went, no lady would consider going without a corset. Indeed, the corset, precisely because it was so restrictive and uncomfortable, was a kind of status symbol. A corset-clad woman could not perform any physical labor. Thus only middle- and upper-class women could wear these hideously confining garments.

For those of us who have trouble with the more remote reaches of a back zipper, the rest of a Victorian woman's garments (separate bodice and skirt, multiple petticoats, bloomers, etc.) would have presented a nearly insuperable challenge. Most women had to don and remove their voluminous and complicated garments alone, often in the small space behind a screen in a corner of the bedroom, since a lady's maid was a distinct luxury.

The final steps, for men and women alike, were the little refinements of grooming: the splash of cologne, the dusting of powder, the adjustment of a brooch. A clean handkerchief in the breast pocket, a final tweak of a curl, and the Victorian lady and gentleman were finally ready to leave the privacy of the bedroom for the more public rooms of the rest of the house or the outside world.

Gold pocket watch and walnut watch stand, late 19th century
PRIVATE COLLECTION

What boy has not peeped with a kind of baffled curiosity into the delicate yet intricate works hidden away in the ancient silver watch which, maybe, is to become his own when he has grown careful enough to be entrusted with so precious a treasure as the family heirloom?

C. L. MATÉAUX, *Wonderland of Work*, 1880

TIME FLIES

Although wristwatches began to be manufactured in the 1850s, they were very slow to catch on. A pocket watch like this one was a badge of middle-class respectability. The Sears catalog of 1900 features six pages of watches for men and women, all in this basic shape (unchanged since the eighteenth century). Women wore their watches attached to a chatelaine or pinned to their bodices. Men carried them in a shallow pocket, with a chain looped across their stomachs.

In the early nineteenth century, a dandy might have had a showy selection of seals and charms hanging from his chain. By the Victorian era, the display had been toned down, but men might still hang the insignia of a fraternal order, for instance, from a watch chain. Harry Houdini, the famous escape artist, had Tiffany make him a watch chain in the shape of handcuffs.

Watches, too, gave men a chance to show some individuality. The cases came in a variety of metals (gold, gold-filled, silver, nickel) and with a variety of ornament, from floral scrolling to an oncoming train. This watch features a shield that could be engraved with the owner's monogram (though in this case it never was). A gold watch like this was an heirloom, and the initials of a previous owner added cachet and sentimental appeal. Given the Victorian mania for specialization, is it any wonder that there were special little pieces of furniture just for overnight watch storage?

ALL BRUSHED UP

The Victorian notion of gentlemen's grooming was a far cry from our eager acceptance of three-day stubble. The way a man was dressed and groomed revealed his social status. And although facial hair went in and out of fashion during the Victorian era (starting with muttonchop sideburns and ending with handlebar mustaches), neatness was always de rigueur.

This dressing set, though strikingly handsome, was not a particularly lavish one. The rustic-looking "bark"-grained bodies are made of a material called "composition," which was an amalgam of sawdust or other fibrous material and a liquid such as shellac or varnish.

The great virtue of composition was that it could be molded into any form. It was also inexpensive. Although the decorative mounts on these dressing tools are silver, they would not have driven up the price by much; the 1900 Sears catalog carried ebony hair- and clothes brushes with similar silver mounts for $1.25.

This may not be a complete set. Although it includes a hand mirror, button hook, and shoe horn, a comb and hairbrush might originally have been included. Men's hairbrushes were either the standard handled brush still used today or the oval military brush (often in pairs) occasionally still found in traditional men's stores. The surviving long-bristled brush was probably intended for hats (the soft bristles would have worked well to brush the deep nap of fur felt), and the rectangular brush is the shape usually used for clothes brushes. Before the invention of dry cleaning, the care of most woolen clothing was based on frequent and careful brushing.

Composition dressing set with silver mounts, probably American, c. 1890
ACCENTS UNLIMITED, LTD.

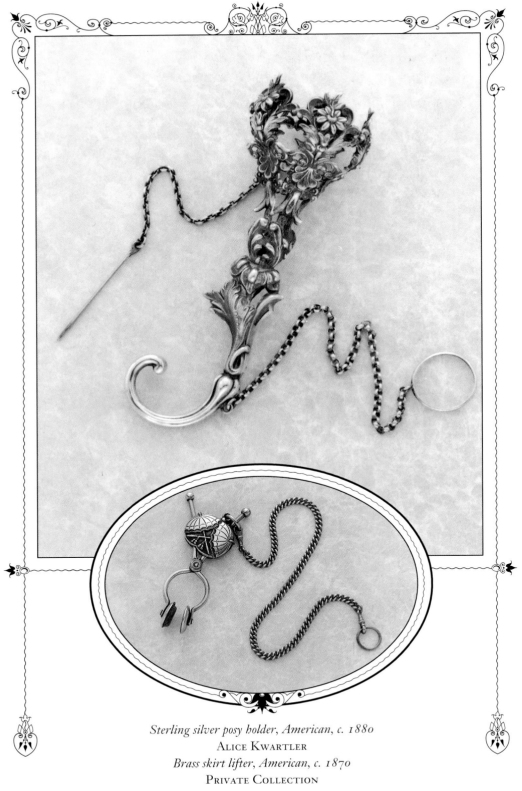

Sterling silver posy holder, American, c. 1880
ALICE KWARTLER
Brass skirt lifter, American, c. 1870
PRIVATE COLLECTION

MANAGEMENT A LA MODE

In an era when ladies' dress was so complex, it stands to reason that ladies had specialized tools to help them manage their clothes and accessories. The chatelaine (see page 130) is one such obsolete article. The posy holder and skirt lifter pictured here are two more.

The posy or tussie-mussie holder is one of the most evocative and charming relics of the Victorian era. Ladies going to dances were given tight little bouquets to carry. They would slip the end into a holder, skewer it with the attached pin so that it wouldn't fall out, and slip the ring over a finger of their gloved hand.

The Victorians made much of flowers as a method of discreet communication. The only gifts a young lady could properly receive from a gentleman were flowers, books, and sweets. Sending a lady a bouquet was a clear token of esteem. In Edith Wharton's *The Age of Innocence* (set in the 1870s) the protagonist, Newland Archer, sends his fiancée a bunch of lilies of the valley every day. The reader realizes he's heading for trouble when he also starts sending yellow roses to another woman.

As well as the general symbolism of admiration and affection, each blossom had a specific significance, and bouquets could be made up to convey a particular message. Popular dictionaries such as *The Language of Flowers* were widely available to help in the translation.

Anyone who has climbed stairs in a long skirt knows that it's easy to trip on the hem. Hence the practicality of the skirt lifter, a decorative little clip on a chain. The clip attached to the skirt, and the lady slipped the ring onto her finger, thus eliminating the possibility of tripping or trailing her skirt on a muddy street.

DOUBLE VISION

America's wealthiest citizens a hundred years ago loved to go to the opera. Attendance there was a chance to demonstrate publicly inclusion in the elite, because box seats could not simply be had for the asking.

In fact, at New York's Academy of Music, boxes were handed down from old family to old family. The new families, with names like Vanderbilt and Whitney, couldn't get a foot in the door, so they built their own competing venue. The Metropolitan Opera opened in 1883, and although its stage facilities were meager, there were rows and rows of boxes, ideal for the display of glorious gowns and magnificent jewels. The first tier was soon dubbed "the Diamond Horseshoe" for its blinding glitter.

The elegant accessories pictured here are indeed worthy of the Diamond Horseshoe. Opera boxes were not situated to provide the best sight lines, so anyone interested in the action on stage (as opposed to the action in surrounding boxes) needed a little ocular help. The scarlet enamel of this pair is unusual; mother-of-pearl was the ordinary material for opera glasses. But in the late-Victorian era, enameled objects such as cigarette boxes and picture frames became very fashionable. Most famously, the Russian jeweler Peter Carl Fabergé took this revival of an eighteenth century French craft to new heights.

The jeweled lorgnette provides visual aid of a different sort. The lenses (which fold at the bridge to fit into the filigree case) magnify, helping the nearsighted to read the program or libretto. This was probably the accessory of an older woman who had the financial resources to pay for such an expensive set of lenses and the nearsighted eyes that required them.

Gold, enamel, and mother-of-pearl opera glasses,
Tiffany and Co., American, c. 1890;
Ivory and silk fan, probably French, late 19th century
PRIVATE COLLECTION
Gold and sterling silver lorgnette with rubies and sapphires, c. 1880
NELSON & NELSON ANTIQUES

Sterling silver chatelaine, Gorham, American, c. 1880
NELSON & NELSON ANTIQUES

GOOD HOUSEKEEPING

The Victorian woman's primary responsibility was running her home, but for a lady of the upper classes this was an executive rather than an operational task. She did not wear an apron and wield a scrubbing brush, but she did hook a chatelaine to the waistband of her dress. And suspended from it were all the tools she would need in a day at home.

The word "chatelaine" comes from the French "château," or castle. A chatelaine is the woman who keeps the castle. One badge of her job is a ring of keys, which is probably the ancestor of this kind of chatelaine.

Like today's Filofaxes, chatelaines could be tailored to a lady's needs. They came in various styles and metals, from gold to cut steel. Sewing implements such as needle or thimble cases were often hung from them, as were keys and mechanical pencils.

On the far left of this example hangs a tiny heart-shaped bottle with a crown on top. This is the usual Catholic representation of the Sacred Heart of Jesus. The container might have been used for smelling salts, a preparation containing ammonia used to revive ladies who fainted. The long, thin bottle next to it might have been a vinaigrette (used to hold vinegar, also to revive the faint) or a scent bottle. The slender tube object is a retractable pencil. A mesh purse hangs at the center, then a tiny memo tablet with ivory leaves, a rough-edged disk for filing nails, and a cylindrical toothpick holder. Everything, in short, that a Victorian lady might need during her daily rounds.

ALL IS VANITY

After the artificiality of the eighteenth century, when powdered hair, lead-based white makeup, and black velvet "beauty spots" were the height of fashion, the pendulum swung back to the naturalistic end of the spectrum. The Victorian lady might wash her face in rainwater and splash some cologne on her wrists, but she was supposed to draw the line at cosmetics.

So what were all the boxes and jars and bottles on her dressing table? Cosmetics, of course. Even the natural look requires a little help.

Powders and creams were scrupulously decanted from their commercial packaging, like everything else in the Victorian house. Vanity or "toilet" accessories were manufactured out of everything from celluloid to gold. The largest bottles might be used for lightly astringent toilet waters like Florida Water or Orange Flower Water. Small jars held cold cream or other face creams. The 1900 Sears catalog advertises "Almond Nut Cream" to reduce wrinkles, a depilatory, and "Secret de Ninon" to remove freckles.

Ladies did admit to wearing face powder, and cylindrical jars or boxes like the one in the inset photograph were often known as "puff boxes." And, since nature does not always put roses on a woman's cheeks, many women also resorted (albeit discreetly) to rouge. The larger jars, often glass with silver lids, were usually called rouge jars, though they were sometimes pressed into service as hair receivers. And, of course, any vanity set included a hand mirror, which a lady would use to check the back of her upswept hairdo.

Sterling silver and cut crystal vanity accessories,
American and English, late 19th century
ALICE KWARTLER
Sterling silver puff box, Tiffany and Co., American, 1886-1890
ILENE CHAZANOF

Transfer-printed earthenware chamber pot, Minton, English, c. 1880
ACCENTS UNLIMITED, LTD.

THE CALL OF NATURE

Although by the late nineteenth century the chamber pot was standard equipment in even the most rustic American outpost, the French king Louis Philippe had found otherwise on a voyage in the southern states in 1797. When he asked for a pot in one house, "We were told that there were broken panes in the windows. . . .The other day, being in a loft, we were looking for the window or other opening that should do service for a chamber pot. We found it ten feet up, and so we insisted on some sort of receptacle; they brought us a kitchen kettle!"

This tale would have horrified the bourgeois Victorian householder. The proper receptacle was a chamber pot like this transfer-printed one, which was made by the famous Minton pottery in England. It may originally have been part of a "toilet set," comprising pitcher and washbasin (like the pair opposite), as well as tooth mugs, soap dishes, and slops jar. The sets might include as many as eight articles, but, given the high mortality rate for pottery, they are rarely found intact these days. Early-American correspondence includes numerous references to households purchasing multiple chamber pots; apparently they were especially likely to be tripped over or dropped (an alarming thought).

In some households, the chamber pot was simply tucked under the bed, but other families preferred to disguise it in a nightstand or a special chair. A few thoughtful housewives somehow decked both pot and slops jar with crocheted covers to stifle the embarrassing noise of pot rattling against jar as it was emptied.

JUST A SPLASH

In no area are we farther from the Victorians than in the department of personal care. Although running water and even fully equipped bathrooms were widespread among wealthy city-dwellers by the end of the century, for most people the basics still took place at a washstand in one's bedroom.

A washstand usually had a waist-height surface that was often covered with marble; there might even be a marble backsplash. On this would be set the ubiquitous pitcher and bowl. Soap, perhaps a sponge, and a towel would be ready to hand on the washstand. Oilcloth was usually spread on the floor before a sponge bath to protect the carpet or flooring.

Of course, water in the pitcher had to be carried to the bedroom, and soapy water from the washbowl had to be hauled away. (The temptation to simply dump the slops out the window was strong and not always resisted.) Needless to say, the daily total immersion that is such a feature of twentieth-century life was highly unusual a hundred years ago.

This handsome bowl and pitcher were manufactured in England using the transfer-printing technique, which permitted the creation of elaborate allover patterns like this one without requiring a great deal of skilled labor.

Earthenware washbowl and pitcher, Copeland/Spode, English, c. 1870
KENTSHIRE GALLERIES

Oak open-twist candlesticks with brass mounts, English, c. 1880;
Brass open-twist candlesticks, English, c. 1870.
KENTSHIRE GALLERIES

JUMP OVER THE CANDLESTICK

Although whale oil and kerosene lamps were widely available in the Victorian era, and gaslight began to illuminate urban homes from the 1850s onward, it would have been foolhardy to abandon candles. Gaslight was unreliable, often leaking and sometimes failing completely. Oil or kerosene lamps required onerous maintenance if they were to provide bright light without smoking and smelling. In houses without numerous servants to perform these tasks, the family would gather around one lamp in the parlor after dinner and light their way to bed with candles. Reading in bed was not an option, nor was lingering in lingerie, for bedrooms were usually quite cold in the winter months.

Not that candles were a perfectly practical light source, either. They were expensive to buy, and many housewives dipped their own, which was smelly, backbreaking labor. The cheapest candles were made of tallow, or rendered animal fat, which tended to soften in hot weather and smell as it burned. (Mice liked it, too.)

Nor was the light of a candle really adequate for sewing or reading. Candles were often stuck in mirror-backed sconces hung on the walls, or placed on the mantelpiece in front of a mirror, to increase their illumination. But large mirrors were expensive and not often found in the middle-class bedroom.

The candlesticks pictured here were probably not meant to be carried from room to room, though the oak pair, with their dished bases, were built to catch any hot dripping wax (a constant irritation of the age). In all likelihood, one would climb the stairs with a chamber light or a go-to-bed (opposite) and light the bedroom candles for the short time it took to get quickly undressed and under the covers.

LIGHT MY FIRE

Although gas lighting was available as early as the 1850s, converting one's house to gas was expensive. Until quite late in the century, most homes were lit by oil or kerosene lamps. Since these lamps were mostly glass and the fuel was liquid, carrying them from one room to another was awkward, if not downright dangerous. So most families took a candle to bed.

The modern-looking candle holder is, surprisingly enough, Victorian. It was probably designed by the Scottish designer Christopher Dresser (see pages 84 and 85). Here, as in most of his rather prescient designs, he has reduced an object to its basic function and its shape to the most simple geometric form. Dresser's chamber light, like more traditional versions, consists of a small platter (to keep hot wax from dripping onto the hand), a lipped tube for the candle, a handle, and a detachable cone-topped cylinder for snuffing the candle out once you get to bed. It also provides storage space for matches under the snuffer. All those elements with no ornament save the ebony rod handle.

The go-to-bed represents a different vein of Victorian design, though its shape is cleverly economical. The container holds matches. When you are ready to go to bed, you pluck one out, light it, and place it in the hole at the top while you negotiate the stairs. (Presumably there is a candle by your bed.) Although go-to-beds have survived the era in some numbers, they may have been more of a decorative accessory than a practical household implement, placed at the bedside but seldom actually used.

Silver plate and ebony chamber light,
attributed to Christopher Dresser, English, c. 1880
SPLIT PERSONALITY
Papier-mâché go-to-bed, probably English, late 19th century
SOOKY GOODFRIEND II GALLERY

Shell-covered paper and fabric box and wall ornament,
English, late 19th century
COLLECTION CECILY BARTH FIRESTEIN

SHE SELLS SEASHELLS

Anyone who has ever scuffed along a beach with his eyes on the sand understands the allure of collecting seashells, but the Victorians had a more elaborate way of using all those shells than dumping them into a jug and turning it into a lamp. Instead, they glued them onto things.

Europeans first became aware of fancy shells in the seventeenth century, when the explorers of the Pacific and Indian oceans brought beautiful exotic shells back to the Old World. Many of them were considered so valuable that they were mounted elaborately in silver or gilt. By the nineteenth century, the first flush of shell collecting had subsided, and shells became materials for yet another Victorian home craft.

Craft shops sold plain boxes or other simple forms (napkin rings or picture frames, for instance). They also sold shells, which probably outnumbered authentic beachcombers' findings on most boxes. The shells were then combined with other decorative materials. The box here sports a green heart-shaped pincushion, a common feature suggesting that shell boxes frequently ended up on the top of a bureau or dresser.

Nautical motifs such as the anchor shape of the wall ornament and the ship picture on the box are frequent. Under the glass dome of the anchor is a tinted photograph, decorated with dried sea grass and shells, of a seaside town. It is probable that some of these seashell trinkets were created as souvenirs from seaside towns. Of course, sentimentality was a frequent component of Victorian crafts as well, and the box with the heart-shaped pincushion features the legend "Remember Me."

SEWING CIRCLE

Thrift and industry were important parts of the Victorian moral code; idle hands, in those days, did the devil's work. When a lady sat in the parlor after dinner with her husband, she would always be working on something.

The nature of that work, of course, varied according to her class. A pioneer housewife on the Plains would have a never-empty workbasket full of socks to darn and clothes to mend. A wealthier woman could consign these mundane tasks to a maid and occupy her fingers with something more "genteel," such as embroidery or crochet. Both women, however, would be more than familiar with the various objects in the larger photograph opposite.

Practical objects of the age were consistently manufactured in elaborate detail with ornate designs. Rich or poor, a lady's sewing tools were a reflection of her good taste. The thimbles and needle cases show the variety of materials possible for even the most mundane of tools. The simple wooden thread spool in the shape of asparagus spears is a typical Victorian visual joke. Objects like it, the acorn thimble case, and the tiny silver basket pincushion very often took the shape of something else, presumably simply to charm and bemuse the user.

The basket in the smaller photograph is not a typical sewing basket, since it is too small to hold the full complement of needlework necessities as well as fabric and threads. It was probably used for a craft that didn't take up much room, such as tatting. The remarkably well-preserved marigold satin lining is elegantly padded and deeply buttoned, just like expensive upholstered furniture of the period.

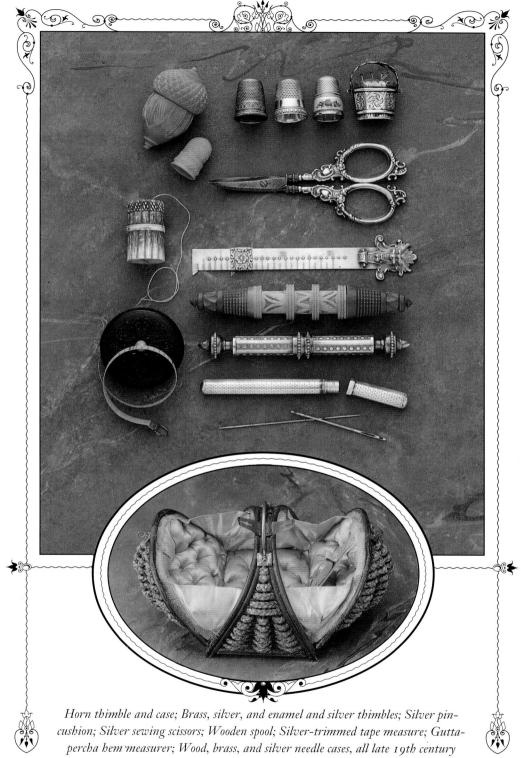

Horn thimble and case; Brass, silver, and enamel and silver thimbles; Silver pincushion; Silver sewing scissors; Wooden spool; Silver-trimmed tape measure; Guttapercha hem measurer; Wood, brass, and silver needle cases, all late 19th century
PRIVATE COLLECTION
Wicker tatting basket lined with satin, late 19th century
HOFFMAN-GAMPETRO ANTIQUES

Sterling silver miniature buttonhooks, manicure tools, and buttonhook;
Sterling silver glove stretcher, Tiffany and Co.; Sterling silver and nickel
curling iron; Sterling silver and horn shoehorn, all late 19th century
PRIVATE COLLECTION

NEAT BUT NOT GAUDY

The Victorian lady may not have worn much makeup, but that didn't mean she neglected her grooming. On the contrary, she took very good care of her hands, her skin, and especially her hair. The elaborate hairstyles of the period required considerable skill and some technology to construct. Curling irons like the one on the bottom row, second from right, were heated over a lamp then used to set curls in the hair.

A hundred years ago, the condition of a woman's hands indicated her social class. The nail file, top right, and the two cuticle tools next to it suggest that hand-care techniques haven't changed in a hundred years for ladies of leisure.

One thing that has, however, is the habit of glove wearing to protect those hands. Victorian women always wore gloves outdoors, even in the hottest weather, and they were also standard attire at all social events. They were usually made of fine kid leather and were supposed to fit so tightly that the shapes of the fingernails were discernible through the kid. The pincers-shaped object pictured second from left on the bottom row is a glove stretcher, designed to help with the task of loosening up new gloves.

Long gloves, like the elbow-length ones worn with evening dresses, had buttoned openings at the wrist. The two tiny implements at the left of the top row are folding miniature buttonhooks, just the right size for taking along in a purse to fasten gloves. The long thin buttonhook at the bottom left could have been used for shoe buttons. The best shoes were dainty, insubstantial affairs, and a shoehorn like the one at bottom right was a help in squeezing a possibly too-substantial foot into the waiting slipper.

BIRTHMARK

One of the activities that took place in the Victorian bedroom that has since been moved to a different venue is childbirth. Giving birth in a hospital is a largely twentieth-century practice; Jimmy Carter, for example, was the first American president who hadn't been born at home.

Birthing scissors like these, in the shape of a stork (reputed, of course, to bring babies), seem to have been part of the childbirth process in the the nineteenth century, but their role is unclear. It was probably only ceremonial. (Note the "secret" carving of an infant in swaddling at the join of the scissors' arms.) The stork's bill does not actually form cutting blades but flat, ridged surfaces that could possibly have been used to clamp the umbilical cord for cutting.

The scissors may also have been used as an iconic good-luck charm, placed in a woman's bedroom while she was pregnant. Perhaps they were passed along from woman to woman, accumulating more totemic force with each successful delivery.

The stork on these scissors is standing on a salamander. Because salamanders, in myth, can live through fire (asbestos used to be known as "salamander's wool"), they symbolize new life. Some birthing scissors show the stork standing on a turtle or tortoise, a common symbol of longevity.

Because childbirth was a painful and dangerous experience in the Victorian era, the salamander on the scissors, with his legendary ability to survive flames, may even refer to the metaphorical trial by fire endured by most Victorian mothers when they gave birth without anaesthesia.

Sterling silver birthing scissors, probably German, late 19th century
NELSON & NELSON·ANTIQUES

Brass-framed hinged mirror with celluloid panel, American, c. 1890
ACCENTS UNLIMITED, LTD.

THROUGH THE LOOKING GLASS

The low dressing table equipped with a mirror as well as a lady's toilet articles appeared in the bedrooms of the wealthy as far back as the seventeenth century. They were quite a luxury, for even dainty little tables took up precious space, and mirrors were extremely expensive. Even as grand a dressing table as the one arranged in 1855 for Queen Victoria's visit to Emperor Napoleon III's palace at St. Cloud only featured a single panel of mirror (topped with a crown and draped with fine lace, to be sure).

A middle-class bedroom of the early nineteenth century might feature one looking glass, hung tilting downward to reflect more of one's figure. By the 1860s, however, techniques for manufacturing plate glass brought mirrors into the price range of the middle class.

Mirrors got larger. Sheets of looking glass were hung over mantels; full-length mirrors adorned wardrobe doors. And it wasn't long before the advantage of hinged mirrors like the one in this photograph became apparent. A lady could see herself from several angles, ascertain that her dress was tidy, and that her hair looked neat all the way around.

The decorative celluloid right panel on the mirror ensured that when the mirror was folded closed it was still attractive. The panel depicts a lady in a sheer white neoclassical gown, surrounded by doves at her feet and in the air. A wide border of flowers frames the picture, creating an idealized feminine image.

STUCK ON YOU

The stickpin was a staple piece of jewelry for both men and women in the Victorian era. In the earlier part of the period, men wore wide, flowing cravats with high-collared shirts. A pin was essential to keep the cravat's slippery folds from coming untied. Later in the century as men's ties narrowed to proportions more familiar to us today, the stickpin (or stock pin, since those wide ties are also called stocks), though less necessary, was not abandoned.

At the same time, women began to wear "tailor-made" clothes, simple skirts and jackets in plain woolen fabrics. A stickpin or two on the lapel of a jacket provided just the right jaunty but modest adornment.

Stickpins were made in every conceivable material. The shanks were usually gold or silver, sometimes twisted to prevent the pin from slipping out. The heads featured gold knots, pearls, cameos, semiprecious stones, animals, fraternal insignia, miniature portraits, hair work, and enamel.

Pins could of course be stored in jewelry boxes but this ingenious silver porcupine made an engaging display of them. It was a common Victorian trick to create functional objects in whimsical, often animal, forms. What makes this holder especially clever is the use of the stickpins themselves as the "quills" of the porcupine. Only when it is put to its proper use is the creature complete.

Sterling silver pin holder with stickpins
in assorted materials, late 19th century
PRIVATE COLLECTION

Fabric-covered porcelain hat pin holder, German, late 19th century;
Hat pins in assorted materials, late 19th century
PRIVATE COLLECTION

HATS OFF

Except for the most formal events, Victorian women covered their heads when they left the house. In the 1860s, they wore close-fitting bonnets that hid the ears and sometimes had a modest frill (called a bavolet) attached to screen the back of the neck. Throughout the second half of the century, bonnets with ribbons that tied beneath the chin coexisted with hats—the scantier and flightier version of headgear that was usually more popular with the younger set.

Though older women tended to cling to the bonnet, by the 1890s hats had become much more prevalent. They came in a wide variety of forms, from tiny curlicues of velvet trimmed with netting, feathers, and flowers, to simple straw boaters. Eventually hats got larger and softer and began to sport overscaled trimmings such as immense fabric flowers and whole stuffed birds.

The larger-brimmed hats had a tendency to blow off in a breeze, and hat pins served as their anchors. These long sharp pins were thrust into the crown of the hat and through the wearer's knotted hair. As Victorian memoirist Gwen Raverat wrote, the result could be painful: "On the top of an open bus, their mighty sails flapped agonizingly at their anchorage, and pulled out one's hair by the handful."

Affluent Victorian women accumulated large collections of hat pins, and consequently required some way to store and display them. Small ceramic hatpin holders were a common sight on the tops of bureaus. Other popular styles were manufactured of cut crystal, fancy glass, or porcelain produced by manufacturers like Limoges and Doulton. This unusual example, made by the Royal Bayreuth company in Bavaria, is covered with rose-printed fabric.

Hand In Glove

The proper Victorian lady was expected to wear gloves at all times, but she couldn't simply pull on any pair that was handy. For each occasion, there were appropriate gloves. Short gloves for the daytime, long gloves for evening, heavier leather gloves for the country; a woman with pretentions to gentility needed a whole wardrobe. A volume entitled *How to Dress on £15 a Year, as a Lady*, stated that a woman needed "six pairs of kid gloves and one pair of double-sewn dog-skin" for a city life, and "only four pairs of kid (including those for evening wear), two double-sewn and two pairs of gauntlets" if she lived in the country.

Gloves were expensive, and the prudent took good care of them, storing their most precious pairs in long glove boxes like this one. Kid, especially the cream shade favored for evening wear (it looked better in gaslight than dead white), showed dirt, and a lady did not wear soiled gloves. As Meg in *Little Women* prepares to go to a dance, she advises her sister Jo, "Gloves are more important than anything else."

Pierced paper glove box; Kid gloves, late 19th century
PRIVATE COLLECTION

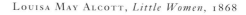

My silk stockings and two pairs of new gloves are my comfort....I feel so rich and sort of elegant, with two new pairs, and the old ones cleaned up for common.

LOUISA MAY ALCOTT, *Little Women*, 1868

FIT TO BE TIED

While women's clothes attained new heights of fantasy, any hint of flamboyance in the masculine Victorian wardrobe was shunned. As a writer in the *Tailor and Cutter* put it in 1871, "A display of order and taste is a pledge that these excellent qualities extend to business transactions and penetrate the manners.... A gay or loud style will as surely give an impression of emptiness and want of reliability."

A dark coat, sober trousers, waistcoat, white shirt, and tie were, by mid-century, the accepted masculine uniform. The details changed but the principles didn't. This restricted wardrobe had to be rigorously cared for if it was to give the required impression of order and reliability. Shirts must be snowy, collars freshly starched, cravats or ties free of wrinkles.

Though men needed fewer gadgets than women to keep their clothes in shape, the tie press in the larger photograph here was an ingenious way to flatten out silk cravats without subjecting them to the potential scorching of the flatiron.

Men's clothes, as well as being simpler, were also much more comfortable than women's. There were also a few ingenious inventions like the brass boot warmer in the inset photograph that further eased their lot. Bedrooms (and the clothes stored in them) were often very cold. A boot warmer filled with hot water could raise the temperature of a pair of boots much closer to 98.6°. This is, however, clearly intended for a large, masculine boot. Perhaps women just had to wear cold shoes.

Inlaid wood and chrome tie press, English, late 19th century
SOOKY GOODFRIEND II GALLERY
Brass boot warmer, American, late 19th century
PRIVATE COLLECTION

BEST DRESSED

Because men's clothes have changed so little since the Victorian era, some of the tools that helped men get dressed a hundred years ago are still with us. Though buttonhooks are now obsolete, shoehorns are still sold in men's haberdasheries (probably only the most meticulous gentlemen actually use them). The two objects at the far right of this photograph are boot pulls. The L-shaped shanks are inserted into webbing loops that are sewn to the inside of the boot; the hooks are then used to pull the boot up onto the leg. They are still very handy for putting on riding boots.

This monogrammed ivory dressing set also includes a glove stretcher. Although the rules about wearing gloves were less strict for men than they were for women, no gentleman would dare go to a dance with bare hands. The notion of bare masculine flesh touching a woman's gloved hand or clothed body was shocking. As a more practical point, no lady would want sweaty handprints on the back of her fragile evening dress. Men's evening gloves, like women's, were white or ivory kid, and they also needed to be stretched before they were put on.

Several of these implements correspond to the lady's dressing tools on page 138, but the simple "masculine" ivory handles contrast with the ornate "feminine" silver handles of those tools, just as masculine clothes contrasted with the more decorative and elaborate feminine wardrobe of those days.

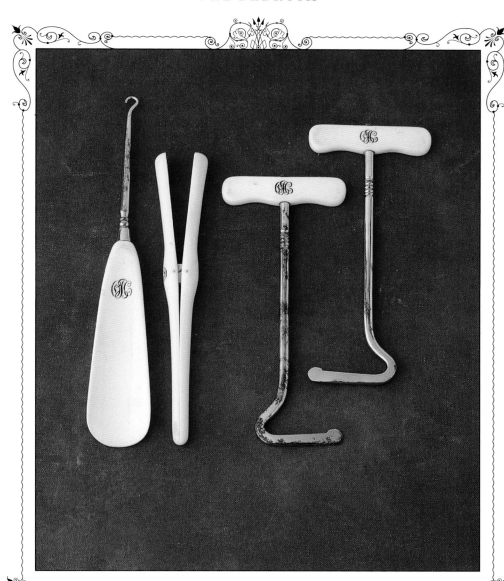

Ivory and silver plate gentleman's dressing set, English, c. 1870
JULIAN GRAHAM-WHITE, LTD.

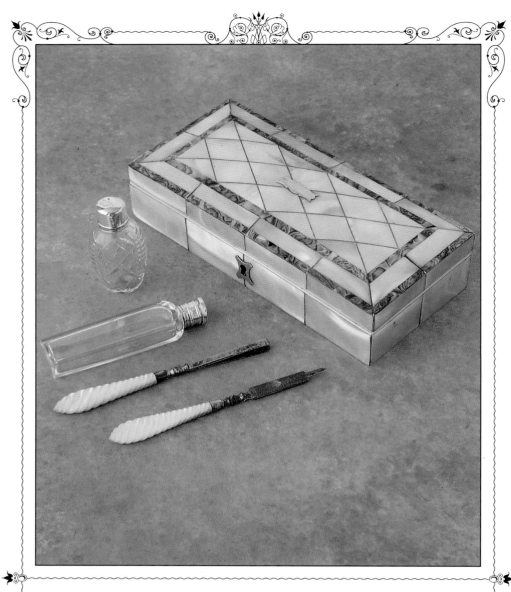

Mother-of-pearl box, fitted with silver-topped glass bottles,
tweezers, and nail file with mother-of-pearl handles, English, c. 1830
JULIAN GRAHAM-WHITE, LTD.

PRECIOUS PEARL

The men's dressing set on page 127, with its bark-like brush backs and handles, represents a conventionally "manly" approach to grooming. This sleek mother-of-pearl toilet set, dating from around 1830, gives us a glimpse of a rather different attitude toward masculine accessories. At that date, the notion of the male dandy was just fading. Though sober coats and trousers had replaced flamboyant silks, men wore embroidered or vividly patterned waistcoats well into the 1830s.

Accessories that gentlemen of the 1860s might regard as effete (rings, multiple watch fobs, ruffled collars and cuffs) were still acceptable. This toilet set, with its silver-topped bottles and grooming tools with mother-of-pearl handles (only the tweezers and nail file are shown in the photograph), reflects a less rugged notion of manliness. Its beautiful materials and workmanship probably earned it heirloom status on a Victorian dresser. It was simply too elegant to discard.

Mother-of-pearl has been highly prized since the sixteenth century, when it first appeared in Europe as the product of Goa, a newly annexed Portuguese colony on the western coast of India. In the nineteenth century, the aesthetic appeal of the material and its exotic provenance (most mother-of-pearl comes from spots such as the South Seas, Panama, and the Persian Gulf) made it very popular for all sorts of uses. For instance, it was frequently used for knife handles (since sets of silver flatware did not include knives until the middle of the Victorian era), buttons, and as decorative highlights in inlaid or papier-mâché pieces.

GOOD SCENTS

In the days before cosmetics companies packaged beauty for us, women often mixed up their own potions. Lola Montez, a celebrated courtesan and "Spanish" dancer (she was actually born in Ireland) of the Victorian era, published a very popular book called *The Arts of Beauty*, which gave recipes for cleansers, lotions, pomades, pastes, and even perfumes.

Eaux de cologne and perfumes were also used for quasi-medicinal purposes in the early nineteenth century: they soothed fever, settled queasy stomachs, even sweetened the breath. But a regulation passed by the Emperor Napoleon III in France separated the medicinal and cosmetic functions. Perfumers caught on quickly and took steps to distinguish themselves from pharmacists.

Proprietary scents, that is to say recognizable fragrances marketed by a single manufacturer, began to appear in the 1870s. Guerlain made a scent called "Eau Imperiale" that was a favorite of the Empress Eugenie. It was sold to other women in a bottle decorated with the imperial crest, an early example of a commercial status symbol.

Even in the 1880s and '90s, when designer Jean-Philippe Worth (son of the couturier Charles) was giving his favorite clients bottles of a house perfume called "Dans la Nuit," the middle-class perfume wearer was probably brewing her scent at home, or buying it from a less than glamorous local drugstore. Like so many other products in the Victorian home, it was decanted before use. Perfume went into an elaborate glass bottle like the two shown here.

Both are fine examples of the flourishing nineteenth-century glassmaking art that delighted in elaborate techniques such as molding, pressing, gilding, etching, engraving, and enameling.

Gilded and enameled glass perfume bottles, late 19th century
PRIVATE COLLECTION

Gilded wood-framed mirrors, c. 1860
PRIVATE COLLECTION

MIRROR, MIRROR

In the twentieth century we tend to take mirrors for granted, but until about one hundred and fifty years ago, they were quite precious. While small glass mirrors were made in the Middle Ages, it wasn't until the sixteenth century that Venetian glass-workers were able to produce larger, more useful mirrors using sheets of blown glass backed with a mixture of tin and mercury.

Improved methods for forming plate glass were introduced in the seventeenth century. Molten glass was poured onto tables rimmed with iron, then rolled to an even thickness. The work was tricky, however, and the results undependable, so mirrors remained extremely expensive.

Because they were so costly, looking glasses were treated with the reverence accorded to paintings or tapestries. They were set in elaborately carved and gilded or painted frames and hung in prominent places. A large mirror hanging over a fireplace was a significant status symbol in the eighteenth century. It also served to reflect light, an important consideration in the age of candles.

Among the myriad inventions and technical improvements of the early nineteenth century was the discovery of a new backing for mirrors: a thin coating of silver that was much safer to work with (and more stable) than the mercury mix. The mechanization of plate-glass manufacture and the 1845 repeal of an English excise tax on glass combined to bring down the cost of mirrors. Finally, the luxury of a looking glass was more widely available.

These two small oval mirrors in their plump flower-decked frames were probably decorative rather than practical. But they would have brought a measure of light and, more importantly, elegance to a mid-Victorian middle-class bedroom.

Copper Works

This mixed-metal bowl was on the cutting edge of fashion when it was manufactured by Gorham in 1884. After the great Centennial Exposition of 1876, the Victorian propensity for the Oriental (especially the Japanese) heated up. Dragons, dragonflies, and paper fans were plastered asymmetrically over porcelains, greeting cards, and metalwork. At the same time, realistic modeling was in vogue, and these three-dimensional applied brass leaves (some with bugs attached) were very up to the minute.

The simple copper bowl displays hammer marks, evidence of the maker's hand, that would have been smoothed over two decades earlier. And the mix of copper, silver, and brass was the latest thing in the 1880s. Since English regulations about silver use forbade its combination with base metals, this Japanese technique was adopted by American but not English metalworkers.

The shallow tray decorated with bats shares several of the same motifs: the hammer marks, the mixed metals, the extremely realistic modeling of the bats. This tray was probably intended for hairpins, though the bats don't exactly smack of the boudoir. They are, however, a reminder of the macabre streak that runs through the Victorian sensibility. This is the culture, after all, that brought us Dracula.

Copper, silver, and brass bowl, Gorham, American, 1884
ILENE CHAZANOF
Copper and silver pin tray, American, c. 1880
ILENE CHAZANOF

Wool paisley shawl, French, c. 1860
LAURA FISHER

PASSION FOR PAISLEY

The paisley shawl is one of the most recognizable relics of the Victorian era, and one that Queen Victoria herself admired.

The pattern that we think of as "paisley" actually originated in the Kashmir region of northern India. The characteristic elongated curling shapes actually represent stylized leaves, flowers, or pinecones. These shawls, which were originally made of the soft hairs of the Tibetan mountain goat (the fiber we know as "cashmere"), were brought to the west by Napoleon, who encountered them during his 1798 conquest of Cairo.

Woolen and silk shawls in these patterns began to be produced by hand in Edinburgh right away. The name "paisley" actually comes from the small town in Scotland that produced many shawls beginning in the early nineteenth century. The finest shawls, sometimes as large as 12 feet by 6 feet, were literally fit for royalty. In 1860 Queen Victoria wrote to her daughter, Crown Princess Frederick of Prussia, suggesting that a shawl would be a good Christmas present for "Grandmama" (Victoria's mother).

The French "four seasons" shawl in this photograph is rather unusual. The russet palette of its deep patterned border is typical, but the four patches of color at the center are not. Each one represents a season, and the wearer would fold the shawl so that the appropriate season's color was displayed most prominently at the back of her neck.

Victorian decorating used an enormous amount of fabric, draped and swagged over tables, couches, and pictures displayed on easels. Expensive paisley shawls were prized possessions, and they were frequently deployed in this manner, adding another pattern to the already lively mix.

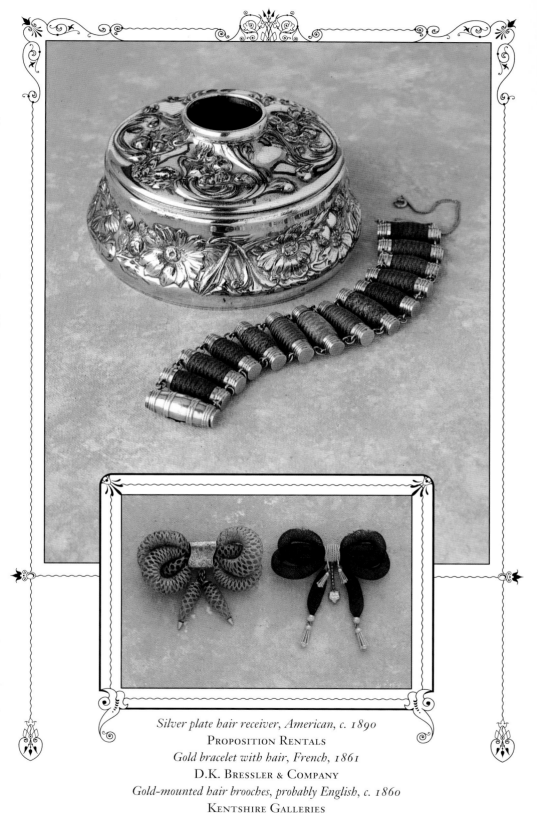

Hair-Raising

One category of decorative objects that makes the Victorian world seem particularly distant from ours is hair crafts. Even parents who have carefully preserved the curls from a baby's first haircut shudder at the thought of braided hair mementos. Our forebears would have had trouble understanding the distinction.

To begin with, the Victorians relished handicrafts, and they employed some improbable media. (Bread sculpture was popular, but for obvious reasons, few Victorian examples survive today.) The Victorians were, moreover, averse to waste, and all women in those days had long hair. As they cleaned their hairbrushes, they tucked the combings into little jars that had lids with circular holes. These hair receivers came in materials ranging from earthenware to the elegant silver repoussé-patterned example pictured here.

The collected hair might be turned into the unfortunately named "rats," little cushions of hair that supplemented the coiffures of ladies whose own locks came up lacking. Or the hair might be fashioned into wreaths or pictures, such as the one on page 41.

Often the hair was knotted into jewelry. Some jewelry featured hair from a departed loved one and was worn to mark a period of mourning. The dark bow in the inset photograph features a tiny gold heart engraved with the name "Arthur." Perhaps his widow wore his hair at her breast.

Other pieces may have been commemorative without specifically being mourning pieces. The bracelet in the larger photograph uses several different shades of brunette hair to form the barrel links. This was probably hair from several different people, possibly members of one family. The bracelet might be analogous to a modern bracelet hung with charms to represent each family member.

Silver plate hair receiver, American, c. 1890
PROPOSITION RENTALS
Gold bracelet with hair, French, 1861
D.K. BRESSLER & COMPANY
Gold-mounted hair brooches, probably English, c. 1860
KENTSHIRE GALLERIES

THE *Nursery*

---◆◇◆---

This is a large family, chiefly of

infantine sons and daughters

(there are 12!) who live in some mysterious

part of the house & are never seen.

HENRY JAMES, *letter to his father,* 1878

---◆◇◆---

Nursery, A. J. Cronin Residence, c. 1915
Museum of the City of New York
The Byron Collection
Background wallpaper design: Schumacher

The room in the Victorian house that has probably been most idealized and romanticized is the nursery. Popular culture, both Victorian and modern, presents us with an image of a cozy, orderly childhood haven ruled over by a firm but benevolent authority. Whimsical toys, punctual meals, and attractive well-behaved children complete the picture. Indeed, many parents today aim for a Victorian look in their children's bedrooms to invoke that apparently secure past. And while memoirs and diaries from the period often contradict this rosy image (some nurseries were grim, some nannies cruel), at least the picture we get from *Peter Pan* or *Mary Poppins* of a self-contained children's world is largely accurate.

Until the beginning of the nineteenth century, children were regarded as small and unruly adults. It wasn't until the optimistic precepts of the Enlightenment sifted into the general population that children were considered innocent (rather than innately wicked) and capable of being trained. The notion of childhood dawned: a special period during which these little creatures were molded into responsible, mannerly, moral beings. Eventually a significant portion of the resources—time, money, space—of every middle-class nineteenth-century family was devoted to the care and education of children.

The Victorian trend toward specialized rooms made a separate nursery a logical allocation of space. So did another pressing concern of the era: health. Childhood mortality rates for the nineteenth century are shocking. As late as mid-century, nearly half of the children born in America or England died before their fifth birthday. Familiar childhood diseases such as measles, mumps, and chicken pox could be fatal. For Victorian parents, with their dawning understanding of how diseases are spread, the notion of a controlled environment had a strong appeal.

The new view of children as impressionable creatures also implied that environment played a part in forming their characters. What they saw around them would form their adult taste. Taste was not, in those days, a relative thing; it had moral implications. Love of vulgarity suggested a degraded character, so children must be brought up to appreciate what was correct. Edith Wharton, in *The Decoration of Houses*, went so far as to say that "the child's surroundings may be made to develop his sense of beauty."

The number of rooms devoted to the nursery varied, of course, according to the wealth of the parents and the size of the family, but the children's area was almost inevitably located on the top floor of the house. Though the Victorians cherished their offspring, they did not hold the modern belief that children required the best of everything. Oddly shaped and poorly lit rooms up three flights of stairs were considered perfectly adequate.

In more modest households, the nursery might be one room furnished for day and night use, but larger establishments had both a "day nursery" and a "night nursery," and even a schoolroom for older children. In fact, the grander the household, the more insulated from adult life the children were. Nanny was the authority, and few mothers would invade her realm without an invitation. Washed, brushed, and dressed in their best, children would visit their

The country Dr. is however a clever man, & the baby was safely born at 1:30 this morning after about 8 hrs labor. She suffered a good deal poor darling, but was very plucky & had no chloroform.

LORD RANDOLPH CHURCHILL, *letter to his mother-in-law, Mrs. Leonard Jerome, on the birth of his son Winston Churchill,* 1874

parents in the formal rooms downstairs for an hour late each afternoon. Otherwise, they spent their days—aside from the walks considered essential for health—in the self-contained nursery realm.

No matter what the scale of the establishment might be, nurseries tended to have certain basic characteristics and furnishings. One of the most notable was the abundance of hard finishes. The developing understanding of epidemiology meant that hangings, carpeting, and any soft goods that might harbor germs must be avoided. Floors were covered with linoleum or cork tile, with perhaps a square of carpet in the center of the room. Curtains might hang at the  window (shades were just as likely), but they would be simple, not the elaborate fringed and tasseled confections that hung in the parlor. Walls were usually whitewashed or wallpapered, and the wallpaper might be coated with varnish to create yet another germ-resistant surface. (Later in the century, papers were manufactured featuring nursery designs by illustrators such as Walter Crane and Kate Greenaway.)

Certain articles of furniture were also standard. A large table, side chairs, and perhaps an armchair or two were necessary. If new, they would probably be made of an inexpensive wood such as white-painted pine. Just as often, pieces considered out of style or too shabby for downstairs would end up in the nursery. More than one Victorian child grew to adolescence kicking the legs of outmoded Chippendale chairs (now worth a fortune) that were banished upstairs as they went out of style.

Shelves or cupboards contained books and toys. Decorating experts usually suggested bookshelves with glass doors, an indication of how carefully books were handled. If children slept and played in the same room, it would also hold beds (white-painted iron bedsteads were considered "hygienic") and a wardrobe for their clothes. If the family's finances could manage it, nursery furnishings would include a piano. Since many Victorian children received their basic education at home from mothers or nannies, nurseries sometimes also doubled as schoolrooms. Globes, blackboards, primers, and maps would join the furniture and playthings.

The sheltered quality of the Victorian nursery is appealing to us today, and so is its orderly nature. Regularity was considered essential to children, so one day followed the next in a predictable routine. Fresh air was deemed important, too, nowhere more than in the newly industrialized cities, so long walks were a daily feature of the schedule. So were rests and extremely simple meals. Children rarely ate the same food as their parents; porridge, boiled mutton, bread and butter, and milk were staples, usually served in small portions. Rich food was avoided because it was thought to "excite the blood."

Attitudes toward child rearing have undergone another major change since the Victorians invented childhood. Today, children are no longer "seen but not heard," and tucked away into their own secluded quarters. Their lives are certainly more exciting than the lives of Victorian children, but certain aspects of the Victorian childhood are still appealing. What modern parent has not wished his children's lives were simpler? What parent hasn't worried about protecting her children's innocence?

One of the most attractive qualities offered by the Victorian nursery was security. Security from need, from danger, from corruption, from all of the uglier realities faced by adults every day. It's no wonder that we cherish the idealized picture of the Victorian nursery, not only as an environment for rearing children, but also, perhaps, as an imaginary refuge for adults.

Wool crib quilt, American, c. 1880
LAURA FISHER

BEAUTIFUL BEDDING

Ingenuity and hard work helped early Americans maximize scarce resources. Some of the resulting techniques, like quilting scraps of fabric together to make bedcovers, produced works of art.

Because fabric was very expensive, bits of cloth from worn-out garments were pieced together and stitched with a layer of padding to create a bed cover. The designs were usually geometric, like the nine-patch pattern on the crib quilt of wool challis shown here. By the late nineteenth century, as the variety of available fabrics became more plentiful, the technique of appliqué gained ground.

Throughout the Victorian period, Englishwomen also produced quilts of geometric and "crazy" design, but quilt-making achieved its apotheosis in the United States. The strong folk traditions of immigrant populations probably contributed to the explosion of creative patterns, while America's tight-knit, far-flung communities kept those traditions alive.

The quilting bee, in which women came together to socialize and to cooperate on finishing their quilting projects, was one of the primary social events in the lives of many rural women. "Album" quilts were often the combined work of several women, each of whom stitched a panel.

Because so much work went into quilts, they were highly prized and often handed down as heirlooms. In spite of the generally fragile nature of fabric, an impressive number of quilts have survived into the late twentieth century.

DOLLY DEAR

Dolls representing children were an innovation of the Victorian period, attributable to a display of wax-headed baby dolls at London's Great Exhibition of 1851 that sparked interest in this new style. By the latter part of the century, the European manufacturers (mostly French and German) who had produced fashion dolls with china heads turned their attention to baby dolls.

Until the 1880s, china heads were sold separately. They were matched to store-bought bodies or attached to a doll body that was made at home. Usually the bodies were soft, stuffed with sawdust or cloth. The invention of "composition"—a moldable substance made up of fillers such as sawdust or flour thickened with varnish, tree sap, or glue—allowed doll-makers to produce stiff bodies with posable limbs.

As the century went on the drive for verisimilitude increased. Faces were quite naturalistically painted, the more expensive dolls featured human hair, and some, like the baby doll here, were made with limbs bent in lifelike positions. The baby doll also has inset rolling eyeballs, known as "flirty eyes."

In the last decades of the century, dolls were often labeled with the names of their manufacturers as well as model numbers. The field is well documented, so it is often possible to arrive at fairly accurate dating for dolls.

Boy doll with china head and composition body,
Armand Marseille, German, c. 1890;
Girl doll with china head and composition body,
Simon & Halbig, German, before 1899
COLLECTION LANCENE LOWELL UNION
Baby doll with china head and composition body,
Kammer & Reinhardt, German, before 1899
COLLECTION LANCENE LOWELL UNION

A Doll's Life

One of our most enduring images of Victorian childhood is that of a large hooded pram being wheeled in a manicured park by a very starchy nanny. In fact, the perambulator was invented in 1848, just in time for the new Victorian habit of cosseting babies (or was its invention prompted by this new tendency?). Before long, a pram was essential equipment for any family that could afford one. It permitted children too small to walk long distances to receive the extended daily doses of fresh air that were considered essential for juvenile health in the era.

Reclining carriages were not introduced until 1880, so this elegant wicker doll pram, which folds down to allow Dolly to take a nap, must have been produced after that date. It is quite a grand toy, big enough to hold a very large doll. Certainly, its occupant was more likely to be a dressy china-headed doll like the ones on page 157 than the modest topsy-turvy doll shown in the inset photograph.

Topsy-turvy dolls, made between 1849 and 1930, were crafted entirely of fabric with painted and glazed faces. The dolls had two heads, two pairs of arms, and a reversible skirt. One of the faces was usually African-American. Topsy-turvy dolls represented a reality that was much closer to the average nineteenth-century childhood than the elegant china dolls. The gingham dress and apron were suitable for the kinds of chores most girls had to perform before they were free to play. Weeding a garden, cleaning vegetables, feeding livestock, and looking after younger siblings were all tasks that might fall to a girl. Her doll, naturally, would lead the same kind of life.

Wicker and cast-iron doll's pram, after 1880
Collection Joy Nagy
Fabric topsy-turvy doll, American, late 19th century
The Victorian Doll Shoppe

TOYLAND

Not many toys have survived from the Victorian era for several reasons, one of which is that by their very definition, toys get hard use. Many of the toys found in antique stores today look battered because they were knocked around for years by small hands. What's more, there were not that many toys in the Victorian nursery to begin with. The abundance and sophistication we take for granted in contemporary children's playthings make the surviving Victorian toys look either charmingly naive, or spare and not very interesting.

The dancing doll in the main photograph was a great commercial success. It was patented in 1864 by James Noe Crow of New York. The loose-jointed doll "dances" when the flexible board that he stands on is tapped. It was such a popular toy that it shows up in a Victorian painting by Eastman Johnson called *The Blodgett Family Christmas Tree*. In the picture, children play with this dancing doll while their mother decorates the family Christmas tree.

While the dancing doll doesn't seem to do very much, the seesaw in the inset photograph may appear even less captivating to adult eyes. But children always enjoy mimicking, with toys, the things they do themselves. The smooth gliding movement of the seesaw was probably as fascinating in this tin toy as it was in real life. Since playgrounds with slides and swings did not exist a hundred years ago, a seesaw was probably a matter of backyard improvisation: a length of wood and a sawhorse or some other fulcrum. The escape from gravity that even a makeshift seesaw provided was no less thrilling a hundred years ago than it is today.

Wooden dancing doll,
American, 1864
HILLMAN-GEMINI ANTIQUES
Tin seesaw toy,
late 19th century
COLLECTION JUDY SINGER

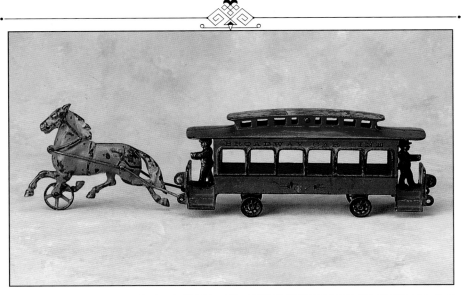

Painted cast-iron Broadway Line trolley, American, c. 1885
HILLMAN-GEMINI ANTIQUES
Painted tin steam train and track, probably German, c. 1880
HILLMAN-GEMINI ANTIQUES

LOVE THAT LOCOMOTION

As it does today, transportation figured as a major theme in Victorian children's toys. And, like today's toys, the most exciting models were those based on the most up-to-date vehicles of the day.

Trolley cars were the first form of urban public transit, and they had a profound effect on the way many urban areas look today. With the establishment of reliable streetcar routes, commuting from an outlying community to a job in the city became possible. When the swifter electric trolley was invented in the late 1880s, suburbs developed farther away from the city center. By the '90s, a network of trolley lines, with their characteristic overhead cables, was a feature of most American cities.

Although the wealthiest Victorians often managed to steer clear of the democratic streetcars and trolleys, trains were universally thrilling. They are still popular toys for children, while for adults, the railroad, a nineteenth-century invention that was itself an agent of enormous change, has become a symbol of the Victorian era. The driving of the golden spike that joined the transcontinental tracks, tall smokestacks belching steam, the lonely whistle of the train as it clattered across the prairie—these images are part of our national consciousness.

This prim little model of a steam train looks a bit frail to carry all that metaphorical baggage. It is actually an example of a plaything called a "parlor toy." These were brought out only on special occasions and played with in the presence of adults. This status may explain why the paint on the engine, coal car and passenger car of this train is still so fresh.

STEAMING ALONG

Before roads or railroad tracks were built across America, transportation of freight and folk took place to a great extent on rivers. And although most of this country's waters are quiet now, a hundred years ago the major rivers were very busy with barges, sailboats, ferries, and steamers. Like the train and trolley that inspired the toys opposite, steamboats were glamorous.

This side-wheel steamer toy was called *City of New York*, after an actual ship that traveled between Manhattan and New Jersey. Although much of the lore about riverboats concerns the flamboyant craft on the Mississippi River, some of the Eastern ships were equally extraordinary in their decor and appointments. Charles Dickens traveled on a Great Lakes steamer that he called "a perfectly exquisite achievement of neatness, elegance, and order." Even for the prosaic trans-Hudson trip, the interiors of some ships were paneled in artistic colors and mirrored throughout.

Many children, however, would be more interested in the dangerous aspects of steamers. Steamship captains (who frequently owned their own ships) were very competitive. If the *Pride of the Highlands* could beat the *Ida Plummer* from Albany to Poughkeepsie, the *Pride* would attract more passengers, and more money would find its way into the captain's pocket. Unfortunately for some passengers, the zest for victory occasionally meant that boilers were overloaded and boats sank. Mississippi steamers ran the further risk of running aground on treacherous river shoals, which provided wonderful inspiration for the kind of disaster-prone fantasy play that children adore.

Painted cast-iron side-wheeler steamboat,
American, late 19th century
HILLMAN-GEMINI ANTIQUES

IRON STEAMBOAT.
No. 64. Fine Iron Steamboat, 16 inches long ....per dozen, $13.50

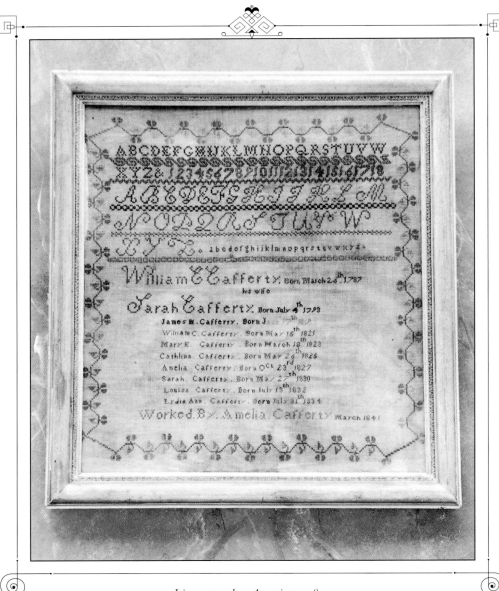

Linen sampler, American, 1841
LAURA FISHER

STITCHES IN TIME

Samplers as showcases for needlecraft skills have been produced since the sixteenth century. Most of the examples created before the nineteenth century consist of a fairly rigid geometric design, usually featuring the alphabet and the name and age of the girl who did the stitchery. Most samplers were worked in tiny, even stitches that the average twentieth-century woman would be hard put to produce.

The sampler shown here states that it was "Worked by Amelia Cafferty March 1841." She was fourteen years old. It includes two alphabets, numbers, and information about Amelia Cafferty's family tree (she was William and Sarah Cafferty's fifth child), all set in a border of stylized flowers.

This is a slightly archaic style for a nineteenth-century sampler. By the time Amelia Cafferty started her embroidery, many girls were turning out more imaginative, pictorial work. Many Victorian samplers feature landscapes complete with houses, farm animals, and rather stiff-looking people. They often include biblical verses or even portray scenes from Scripture such as Noah's ark or the flight into Egypt.

Most disconcerting to modern eyes are the gloomy sentiments that sometimes appear. In 1863, an eighteen-year-old Welsh girl named Anne Thomas worked a sampler gaily covered with flowers, birds, and butterflies. At the top, minute cross-stitches spell out this verse:

In the cold Grave this Frame must rest
And Worms shall feed on this poor Breast
These Hands shall then be Useless Grown
And I alas no more be known
No more these feet shall ever walk
No more this tongue shall ever talk.

BIG BEAUTIFUL DOLL

Dolls in the Victorian era were not always intended for children. In the period before the launching of fashion magazines, fashion dolls often brought news of styles to eager customers. These dolls were clothed in the latest modes and circulated among their customers by ambitious dressmakers. The dolls themselves were often manufactured in France or Germany. Their glazed china heads and limbs were attached to a soft stuffed body. Some of them even featured elaborately styled human hair.

Although fashion dolls ended up in the nursery as well, the level of refined detail on many of them was better appreciated by adults. The doll pictured here is twenty inches high, rather large for a small child to play with. Her features and hair are painted on, as is a pink garter on one of her legs. Her clothing is beautifully made, from hand-tucked bloomers to the lace trim on the sleeves of the detachable bodice. Even the pattern on her dress is in appropriate scale to her diminutive height.

Fashion doll with china head and limbs,
probably German, c. 1875
THE VICTORIAN DOLL SHOPPE

Horsehide and wood horse pull toy,
probably German, c.1890
HILLMAN-GEMINI ANTIQUES

HORSING AROUND

To many twentieth-century children, a horse is as exotic as an animal in a zoo. But a hundred years ago, horses were part of the everyday world, and their charm as toys was the charm not of the exotic, but of the familiar.

For much of the century, motorized transportation was the thrilling exception and travel behind a horse was the rule. Why else would the strength of an engine be measured in horsepower? Horses pulled not only carriages but also barges, wagons, and sleighs. The ability to handle a horse was taken for granted in rural areas, where equine effort was essential to producing crops.

In cities, horses pulled cabs, trolleys (see page 160), and delivery wagons, and muddy streets were made extremely hazardous by the constant addition of manure. One of the earliest objections to motorcars was that they made too much noise. Their loud engines frightened skittish horses who had a tendency to shy or bolt, with disastrous results for their passengers or freight.

Horses of all descriptions were common occupants of nurseries, but the best ones, like the horse in this photograph, were covered with actual horsehide. This is a very lifelike steed, with a flowing mane and tail, bright eyes, and flaring nostrils.

PENNY WISE

Thrift was a trait the Victorians valued highly, and savings banks were an admirable way to pass the moral concept along to children. The five banks in the inset photograph are quite small: the tallest is not even five inches high. A penny was worth quite a bit in those days, so juvenile fortunes didn't take up a lot of room.

The banks are all made of cast iron (it presumably provided a measure of security for the funds) and were originally painted in bright colors. Several of them are actually miniature bank buildings, complete with windows to monitor the savings progress. Some real savings institutions gave these small banks (emblazoned with their own names) to their important depositors to encourage the younger generation in good financial habits.

Bank-shaped banks projected an image of security, but the cast iron trick pony bank made saving much more fun. A penny is inserted in his mouth. When the depositor presses a lever on the base, he dips his head to drop the penny into the manger in front of him. Funds accumulate in the base, which is hollow. Novelty banks of this kind were very popular late in the century and often featured clever actions such as William Tell shooting the apple off his son's head with a penny.

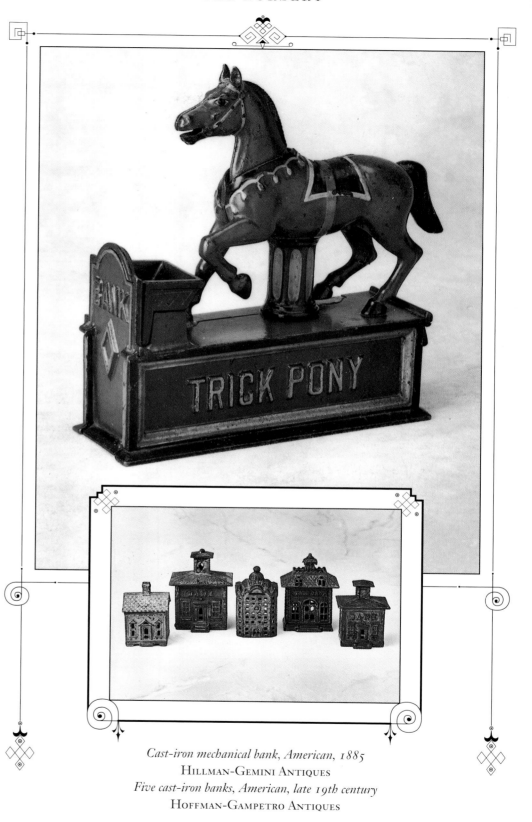

Cast-iron mechanical bank, American, 1885
HILLMAN-GEMINI ANTIQUES
Five cast-iron banks, American, late 19th century
HOFFMAN-GAMPETRO ANTIQUES

Plush kitten figurines,
German, late 19th century
COLLECTION LANCENE LOWELL UNION

FELINE FRIENDS

Most Victorian children did not play with stuffed animals. Although a few stuffed toys were produced during the nineteenth century, the plush bears named for President Theodore Roosevelt ("Teddy" bears) in the early twentieth century were the first widely popular stuffed animals.

These tiny plush kittens are an ornament rather than a toy, and their pristine condition attests to the fact that small fingers rarely played with them. Their lifelike poses and playful air no doubt added to their appeal. Cats were popular pets in the Victorian era, as they are now, as much for their ability to keep rodents under control as for their easy, graceful companionship.

This feline family was manufactured in Germany, where many of the world's best toys have long been produced. (The dolls on page 157 were made in Germany as well.) The famous Steiff company, renowned for its naturalistic stuffed toys, still exports many plush creatures to America.

A number of factors probably contributed to German supremacy in toymaking. One was the great natural resources: the heavily forested mountains of central Germany, known as the Thuringer Wald, provided wood for whittling and carving. A strong sculptural tradition also survived from the Middle Ages. Finally, Teutonic folk tradition produced fantastic tales, many of which, collected by the Grimm brothers in the nineteenth century, form the basis of our fairy tales. After all, Snow White appeared first in Germany as "die Schneewitzchen."

LITTLE TREASURES

As many a parent found long before the Victorian era, silver is a very practical material for implements that a baby will use. It may dent but it never breaks, and many families have long traditions of passing baby cups or rattles from one generation to the next.

Although the world is almost completely transformed in every respect since the seventeenth century, babies three hundred years ago also played with rattles. They were often made of a branch of coral, just the right shape for fretful infants to suck or chew. The silver mounting usually featured tiny bells that glittered and jingled when the rattle was shaken in a baby's fist.

The rattle here, much simpler in design, is lollipop shaped with a relief of a rabbit on one side. Rabbits, with their soft fur and obliging natures, are often associated with nurseries. Beatrix Potter's classic children's tale, *Peter Rabbit*, was not published until 1902, so despite this rabbit's Potterish look, he probably predates Peter.

The spoon and fork at the center of the photograph, with short child-sized handles, were made by the American silversmiths Kirk & Son in an elaborate repoussé style similar to one that Kirk produced in adult sizes. Even the smallest children could thus learn early to appreciate elegance.

At far right is a mother-of-pearl teething ring in a classic style, with a small bell hung from it. The bell shows a baby whispering something in the ear of a grinning man in the moon. Below the moon is engraved the legend, "Baby Secrets."

Sterling silver rabbit rattle, Webster, American, late 19th century;
Sterling silver spoon and fork, Kirk & Son, American, late 19th century;
Mother-of-pearl and sterling silver teething ring,
Webster, American, late 19th century
ALICE KWARTLER

FOR MINIATURE MANSIONS

Very small furniture has been produced for several hundred years. Before there was any thought of letting children play with it, cabinetmakers made miniatures of their wares to use as sales models. These little chairs and chests of drawers, ingeniously detailed, are now collected by adults.

Indeed, the first model houses built to a small scale were most likely intended for grown-ups. At Nostell Priory, a country house in England, there is a grand three-story doll's mansion crafted in the middle of the eighteenth century, reputedly by the master cabinetmaker Thomas Chippendale. Its exalted provenance, however, fades to insignificance beside the charm of its furnishings, from grand canopied beds in velvet and silk down to a glass mouse skittering beneath the kitchen table.

Few adults or children can resist the lure of miniaturization. The details of these tiny articles—drawers that really open and kettles that really pour—and the skill that turns a scrap of chintz into a mock-tapestry carpet enchant viewers of all ages.

This engaging suite of furniture exhibits the same allure. Fine fringe has been used to simulate the rich, heavy trim so fashionable in the 1860s and '70s, while the fabric with its tiny starbursts reads as deeply buttoned upholstery, stylish at that time. The balloon-shaped chair backs and low arms (to allow for a lady's spreading skirts) are also typical of the period.

The two dolls perched on the furniture are sitting as primly as if the young man were paying a first call on the grandly dressed young lady. The little china dog, perfectly scaled, adds a lively touch to the table and chairs set that completes the furniture suite.

Cotton and wood suite of doll parlor furniture, probably French, c. 1875; Girl doll with china head, late 19th century; Boy doll with china head, c. 1850; China dog, late 19th century
THE VICTORIAN DOLL SHOPPE

LET'S PLAY HOUSE

While some small Victorian furniture, like the parlor suite on the opposite page, was meant for dolls, other pieces were probably intended to be played with independently. This mahogany drop-leaf desk is seven inches high, and therefore could only be accommodated in the largest of doll's houses.

The creator was able to build many cunning details into this desk. The simple, blocky style of the piece is not especially Victorian, but rather harks back to the eighteenth century, when a many-drawered chest with a drop leaf like this one was known as a "secretary." The architectural detailing at the center of the piece, with two pillars flanking a hollow arch, is also related to typical eighteenth-century styles, as are the simple bracket feet. This is the kind of furniture, in fact, that might well have been relegated to a nursery if it was too well-made to discard but too plain to be fashionable. A little girl playing with the small version might have recognized its kinship with a similar piece in her own nursery. Certainly, the vases on their little lace doily add an inimitably Victorian touch.

The tureen and candelabras would add a gracious note to any dollhouse dining room. The tureen, with matching ladle, may be from Staffordshire, England, like the plaques on page 40 and the cat and dog figures on page 23. Since soup was served as a prelude to almost every Victorian dinner, a tureen was an important element of fine dining, for dolls and humans alike.

Mahogany drop-leaf desk, American,
late 19th century
COLLECTION JOAN McELROY
Earthenware tureen and pewter candelabras,
possibly English, late 19th century
THE VICTORIAN DOLL SHOPPE

Kind collectors and dealers loaned their treasures for the photograph opposite the title page of this book. Some of these objects and many similar ones are pictured and described in greater detail within the pages of the book.

FIRST ROW FROM TOP:
Bronze watch stand and silver watch
PRIVATE COLLECTION

Doll in crocheted dress
COLLECTION JOY NAGY
Doll in blue dress with composition body and china head
PRIVATE COLLECTION

Brass footed box with pietra dura panels; Bronze cherub figure
PRIVATE COLLECTION

Embossed leather photo album
ACCENTS UNLIMITED, LTD.
Vienna bronze bulldog statue
HOFFMAN-GAMPETRO ANTIQUES

Cast-iron friction car
HILLMAN-GEMINI ANTIQUES

SECOND ROW FROM TOP:
Sterling and crystal perfume bottle
HOFFMAN-GAMPETRO ANTIQUES

Black cut glass perfume bottle
PRIVATE COLLECTION

Cast-iron mechanical bank
HILLMAN-GEMINI ANTIQUES

Ceramic and brass powder box
PRIVATE COLLECTION

Bronze and marble thermometer stand
PRIVATE COLLECTION

Bull's eye condenser magnifying glass
ANTIQUE CACHE
Coddington lens magnifying glass
LYME REGIS, LTD.

THIRD ROW FROM TOP:
Miniature tin condiment set
ACCENTS UNLIMITED, LTD.

Lusterware and gilded enamel pitcher
ACCENTS UNLIMITED, LTD.

Sterling silver porcupine stickpin holder
PRIVATE COLLECTION

Sterling silver and cut glass perfume bottles
PRIVATE COLLECTION

Spongeware pitcher and jar
COLLECTION KATHRYN LICHTER

FOURTH ROW FROM TOP:
Porcelain cup and saucer
BARDITH LTD.

Parian ware bust of Sir Walter Scott and tartan-covered miniature books
LYME REGIS, LTD.

Sterling silver puff box, Tiffany and Co.
ILENE CHAZANOF

Glass weights
COLLECTION ANITA SAULINO WOLFSON

Silver plate sugar bowl
COLLECTION KATHRYN LICHTER

Many dealers and shop owners were generous and helpful in loaning objects for inclusion in this book. Information about their businesses is included here to aid readers and collectors.

As all Victoriana lovers know, New York City is a mecca for collectors and dealers alike. Of particular note is one especially convenient "shopping center." The Manhattan Art & Antiques Center (1050 Second Avenue, New York, N.Y. 10022) is a three-story building housing one hundred individually operated shops offering period furniture, jewelry, silver, Americana, and Oriental and African art from several historical periods. Many of our contributors are housed there. We thank them and all the other dealers who contributed to this book.

ACCENTS UNLIMITED, LTD.

Decorative objects, furniture, chandeliers, silver, and jewelry. Particular emphasis on the unusual and the eccentric. Special searches done. 360 Amsterdam Avenue, New York, N.Y. 10024. Telephone: (212) 580-8404. Letter and phone inquiries welcome.

ALICE KWARTLER ANTIQUES

A wide array of fine objects in sterling, crystal, and enamel, including picture frames, vanity accessories, Tiffany and Co. silver, cuff links, and jewelry. Baby and bridal registry service available. 125 East 57th Street, New York, N.Y. 10022. Telephone: (212) 752-3590.

ANTIQUE CACHE

An extensive collection of desk accessories, including inkwells, pens, paper clips, magnifying glasses, bookmarks, and blotters. Plus a large selection of twist candlesticks and bamboo furniture. 1050 Second Avenue, Gallery 64, New York, N.Y. 10022. Telephone: (212) 752-0838.

BARDITH LTD.

Specialists in eighteenth- and nineteenth-century English, European, and Chinese export pottery and porcelain. A large and notable collection of eighteenth-century glassware, plus dinner, tea, and coffee services. 901 Madison Avenue, New York, N.Y. 10021. Telephone: (212) 737-3775.

BARR-GARDNER ASSOCIATES, LTD.

Decorative objects and furniture of the eighteenth and nineteenth centuries. "Grand Tour" items and "after-the-antique" marbles and bronzes. Embellishments for the garden, plus Venetian glass fantasies and stemware. 125 East 57th Street, New York, N.Y. 10022. Telephone: (212) 838-2415; Fax: (212) 355-6031. Inquiries welcome.

BAUMAN RARE BOOKS

Books, autographs, and leather-bound sets in all fields, including literature, Americana, science, medicine, history, travel and exploration, and children's illustrated books. New York: The Waldorf-Astoria, Lobby Level, 301 Park Avenue, New York, N.Y. 10022. Telephone: (212) 759-8300. Philadelphia: 1215 Locust Street, Philadelphia, Pa. 19107. Telephone: (215) 546-6466; Fax: (215) 546-9064. Catalogues issued regularly by the Philadelphia office.

CLIFFORD BARON

Unusual jewelry from the 1920s through the 1950s. Objets d'art and collectibles from the nineteenth and twentieth centuries. 1050 Second Avenue, Gallery 18, New York, N.Y. 10022. Telephone: (212) 355-0767.

D. K. BRESSLER & COMPANY

Antique and estate jewelry, with particular emphasis on Victorian and Edwardian pieces. Plus silver and bronze objets d'art. 10 West 47th Street, Booth 33, New York, N.Y. 10036. Telephone: (212) 302-2177. For private appointments: (212) 601-6136.

E. BUK

Period and historical furniture, architectural renderings, and ephemera. Specializing in antique scientific, mechanical, medical, nautical, and technological objects, instruments, and devices. 151 Spring Street, New York, N.Y. 10012. Telephone: (212) 226-6891. Appointment advisable.

HILLMAN-GEMINI ANTIQUES

Specializing in antique toys, mechanical penny banks, and American folk art, including weather vanes, wooden sculpture, and folk paintings. Emphasis is placed on the period 1850 to 1935. 927 Madison Avenue, New York, N.Y. 10021. Telephone: (212) 734-3262. Letter and phone inquiries welcome.

HOFFMAN-GAMPETRO ANTIQUES

Antique furniture and decorative objects, with particular emphasis on fine silver, period jewelry, and collectors' items. 1050 Second Avenue, Galleries 37 and 91, New York, N.Y. 10022. Telephone: (212) 758-1252.

ILENE CHAZANOF DECORATIVE ARTS

An extensive and affordable collection of late nineteenth- to mid-twentieth-century decorative objects. Primarily European and American silver, metalwork, ceramics, glass, and accessories. Retail, wholesale, rentals, and research. By appointment only. 7 East 20th Street, New York, N.Y. 10003. Telephone: (212) 254-5564.

IRIS BROWN'S VICTORIAN DOLL & MINIATURE SHOPPE

Specializing in antique dolls, doll clothes, dollhouses, and doll furniture. 253 East 57th Street, New York, N.Y. 10022. Telephone: (212) 593-2882.

JULIAN GRAHAM-WHITE, LTD.

Two floors of whimsically displayed accessories and furniture from the eighteenth and nineteenth centuries. Specializing in eccentricities such as walking sticks, newel-post knobs, needlework cushions, crystal bibelots, and occasional tables. 957 Madison Avenue, New York, N.Y. 10021. Telephone: (212) 249-8181; Fax: (212) 249-8989.

KENTSHIRE GALLERIES

Eight gallery floors of beautifully displayed English furniture and accessories dated 1690 to 1870. Plus an extraordinary collection of antique and period jewelry, including Victorian, Edwardian, Art Deco, and retro pieces. Main gallery: 37 East 12th Street, New York, N.Y. 10003. Telephone: (212) 673-6644; Fax: (212) 979-0923. Boutique: Bergdorf Goodman, 7th floor, Fifth Avenue at 57th Street, New York, N.Y. 10019. Telephone: (212) 872-8652.

KURLAND · ZABAR GALLERY

English and American decorative arts, dated 1840 to 1940. Specializing in Gothic, Renaissance, and Egyptian revivals, plus the Aesthetic and Arts and Crafts movements. 19 East 71st Street, New York, N.Y. 10021. Telephone: (212) 517-8576.

LAURA FISHER ANTIQUE QUILTS AND AMERICANA

The nation's largest selection of antique quilts, hooked rugs, woven coverlets, paisley and Amish shawls, Beacon blankets, and assorted vintage textiles. Plus a sampling of decorative accessories and American folk art. 1050 Second Avenue, Gallery 84, New York, N.Y. 10022. Telephone: (212) 838-2596.

LINDA HORN ANTIQUES

An eclectic selection of fine decorative objects and tableware, with particular emphasis on late nineteenth-century English accessories. 1015 Madison Avenue, New York, N.Y. 10021. Telephone: (212) 772-1122.

LYME REGIS, LTD.

A cozy little shop featuring an assortment of nineteenth-century eccentric small decorative objects that are often other than what they seem. 68 Thompson Street, New York, N.Y. 10012. Telephone: (212) 334-2110. Letter and phone inquiries welcome.

MAN-TIQUES LTD.

Specializing in American and English antiques of particular appeal to men, including desk accessories, smoking and bar accessories, scientific instruments, and decorative objects. 1050 Second Avenue, Gallery 51, New York, N.Y. 10022. Telephone: (212) 759-1805.

NELSON & NELSON ANTIQUES

A wide selection of fine silver, glass, and enamel decorative objects, with particular emphasis on late nineteenth-century English and European bibelots and jewelry. 1050 Second Avenue, Gallery 58, New York, N.Y. 10022. Telephone: (212) 980-5191.

PROPOSITION RENTALS

A rentals-only prop house specializing in antique and period tabletop objects that caters to the advertising, television, and theatrical industries. Particular emphasis is placed on turn-of-the-century and early twentieth-century objects. 118 West 22nd Street, New York, N.Y. 10011. Telephone: (212) 929-9999.

SOOKY GOODFRIEND II GALLERY

Tabletop decorative objects and "secondary" jewelry. Particular emphasis is placed on brass and glass inkwells, brass picture frames, papier-mâché objects, and agate and silver jewelry. Open to the wholesale trade and serious collectors. P. O. Box 20115, New York, N.Y. 10028. Letters of inquiry welcome.

SPLIT PERSONALITY

Jewelry and decorative objects in metal and glass, with particular emphasis on Arts and Crafts, Jugendstil, and Art Nouveau items. Specializing in Liberty & Co. and Christopher Dresser objects. P. O. Box 419, Leonia, N.J. 07605. Telephone: (201) 947-1535.

THE VICTORIAN DOLL SHOPPE

See Iris Brown's Victorian Doll & Miniature Shoppe.

YALE R. BURGE ANTIQUES

An extensive selection of fine English, French, and Oriental antique furniture, lamps, mirrors and decorative accessories. 305 East 63rd Street, New York, N.Y. 10021. Telephone: (212) 838-4005.